Kate O'Donnell is a writer, editor and bookseller specialising in children's and young adult literature. She has a BA in History and French from the University of Melbourne and studied Professional Writing and Editing at RMIT. Her first novel, *Untidy Towns*, was shortlisted for the Indie Book Award and the Readings Young Adult Book Prize in 2018. *This One is Ours* is her second novel.

Also by Kate O'Donnell

Untidy Towns

THIS ONE IS OURS

KATE O'DONNELL

UQP

First published 2020 by University of Queensland Press
PO Box 6042, St Lucia, Queensland 4067 Australia

uqp.com.au
reception@uqp.uq.edu.au

Cover design by Astred Hicks, Design Cherry
Cover image by Tinxi/Shutterstock
Author photograph by Victoria Scott Photography
Typeset in 11/15 pt Bembo Std by Post Pre-press Group, Brisbane

Printed in Australia by McPherson's Printing Group

The University of Queensland Press is assisted by the Australian Government through the Australia Council, its arts funding and advisory body.

A catalogue record for this book is available from the National Library of Australia.

ISBN 978 0 7022 6028 5 (pbk)
ISBN 978 0 7022 6172 5 (epdf)
ISBN 978 0 7022 6173 2 (epub)
ISBN 978 0 7022 6174 9 (kindle)

University of Queensland Press uses papers that are natural, renewable and recyclable products made from wood grown in well-managed forests and other controlled sources. The logging and manufacturing processes conform to the environmental regulations of the country of origin.

Pour Emmanuelle, Katline, Tony et Kevin.

1

This is the story of me (Sofie) and the time I went to France in search of art and romance and a dream.

Before I went to Paris, I'd searched for the same things at home. There is a creek not far from my house (my parents' house in the suburbs of Melbourne, Australia), and when you walk along it, the light that filters through the leaves is sparkly and green. There are usually some muddy-pawed dogs bounding along, and all kinds of people wandering. We're not supposed to go down after dark, because of Stabby Joe and his screwdriver, though sometimes I go after dark anyway, and here are three reasons why:

1. I love the night-time.
2. It's almost frighteningly quiet (which is adrenaline-rushing).
3. There isn't anyone around (apart from potentially Stabby Joe, and I think he's just a rumour). I stick to the shadows, flitter like leaves falling from trees.

Our house isn't so noisy anymore because there's just me and Mum and Dad living there since Hana moved out, but it's a small house and everyone knows where everyone else is most of the time. And so I love walking because when I walk, I walk alone, and I am free to go where I want, literally as well as in my mind.

It's probably about fifteen minutes from our house to the creek, but I don't really care about time this afternoon. I'm on the search for tiny beautifuls. For lines in the world I can mimic on paper, with pencil, with paint. The shape of a leaf, with lovely veins that are perfect for capturing with the just-sharpened tip of a pencil. A hard, grey, knobbly gumnut, whose surface is textured in a way I hope I can one day re-create on paper. A meandering crack in the concrete footpath that will be the start of something abstract. Abstraction is not my strong point, but I feel its pull. Something tiny. Something beautiful.

There's a soft hedge at the end of my street, and this is where I run my fingers along the foliage, and where I turn left towards the creek. I'm hardly conscious of it as a route marker, not really; only conscious of the familiar feeling of my fingertips on cool, thin leaves. Is this what habit is? Hardly noticing things?

Usually when I am walking, I am dreaming. Most of my daydreams revolve around romance and art and how badly I want both of those things. And soon, once I'm in France, I will be able to walk in places I've only been to in my mind.

Sometimes I settle into an old dream just to relive it and it's fascinating when it comes out different – maybe I've walked a slightly different route that day.

I move to New York City for a fancy job and I live in

a rich person's opulent apartment and throw parties that only the most intriguing people attend.

I go to university to study Fine Arts, and everyone finds my final project so impressive that my work is chosen to hang in the National Gallery.

Or maybe I step along the wonky stone steps down one side of the creek, my shoes tapping out a pattern, and I accidentally lose my footing and slip right into the creek! The water is chilly and I sit there, half submerged. A dog barks. A boy's face peers down at me and he asks, 'Are you all right?' He reaches out a hand and I take it …

Sometimes the boy and I don't even kiss, but just lie in the long grass together while my dress dries off. Sometimes the dog pulls me out of the creek like a canine hero and lies with us in a sunny patch – good doggo.

I've filled most of a sketchbook drawing two pairs of feet in long grass covered with wildflowers. Feet are hard, but I've had a lot of practice. It's funny to think about feet, and I don't think I'd want to touch feet with just anyone – it feels too intimate. Too intimate for me, little miss sweet sixteen never been kissed.

Picnics are a romantic thing.

You see? I can't stop dreaming.

Have you ever heard a song so beautiful and meaningful that for three minutes everything is right with the world?

That is how I want to feel all the time.

In art class, time slows, and I create moods and worlds with my pen and my brush.

In Paris, everyone loves art, I'm sure of it. It's a city full of artists, through history and even now. Probably because of the light. It's the city of that, too. And, as you learn as you become an artist, light is essential when creating art.

I've read the English translation of Arthur Rimbaud's poem *Roman* many, many times. (*On n'est pas sérieux, quand on a dix-sept ans – You aren't serious, when you're seventeen*). It is a very romantic poem. I picture myself beneath the lime trees and imagine my mad, even less serious, sixteen-year-old heart going Crusoeing through all the romances. Oh! I cannot wait for the romances!

I have dreamed of art and love and beauty since forever and now … now, I am no longer dreaming. Now, I am going to Paris, France.

Back at my house, Crow's waiting for me, leaning against the fence, her tights ripped above her boots.

'You know you can go in even if I'm not here,' I say as we walk together to the front door. 'My parents don't mind.'

She just shrugs, tossing her long, dark tangles over her bony shoulder. We've been friends since prep – ten whole years – and she still acts like a newcomer when she comes around to mine.

'I was just reading this thing,' she says. 'There's just no way the government is going to reduce emissions and meet the targets for 2030. We're screwed.'

'No, we're not,' I say reassuringly. 'They won't let it happen.'

Crow has this scowl she does. 'I hope you're right,' she says, but the scowl is really saying *you're wrong*. Crow's told me what could happen if the earth warms two degrees. But I try not to believe her. I'm an optimist.

I can hear voices as we go inside – Mum, Dad, and Hana. 'It's bad enough I have to wear these,' Hana is saying in a grumpy tone. 'I don't want to then buy *new* boring grey outfits every month or two.'

'You could buy a washing machine,' Dad suggests, as though Hana's being dim. 'Then you wouldn't be taking over ours all the time.'

My sister comes over to do her washing most weeks. Hana's ten years older than me and she lives in a scungy share house with a group of fascinating friends who all seem to love each other deeply and irritate each other frequently. She's happy there, but is annoyed by the way their old half-broken-down washing machine leaves brown flecks all over her work clothes. I know Dad loves that she visits so much though.

'Sof!' Hana squeezes me in a tight hug. 'Hey, Crow. How's your gran?'

'Yeah, she's good,' replies Crow, while I scrub my hands at the kitchen sink and try to wash away that layer of worry … *emissions, coral, sea levels, food security.* I dry my hands on the tea towel, roll it and flick it at Hana, who grabs it and flicks it back.

'How are you, Caroline?' says Mum. Crow just nods. Mum's always trying to get Crow to like her. It's not that Crow *doesn't* like her (my mum's good people), but maybe if she called her by her proper name …

'Hey, carry this,' says Hana, handing me the salad bowl and hustling us all to the table. Tonight, it's all my favourite foods: complicated salad with lentils and grains and herbs and yoghurt dressing, accompanied by fish and chips from the place around the corner. They always put in an extra potato cake. *Bon appétit!*

'So Claudine and her husband are meeting you at the airport?' asks Dad, rolling the pepper grinder across to Mum and scattering pepper everywhere (Dad likes to try things a different way whenever he can).

'It's Claudette,' I correct him for the seventeenth time. 'And Léon.'

'And the daughter, Delphine,' adds Crow.

'Yup. I don't know if she's coming to the airport though.'

Honestly, Crow has the most astonishing memory. She'll say, 'Remember Ella's birthday party in year three?' and I'll say, 'Yes!' but my memories are *cake/Ella's mermaid t-shirt/lolly bag*, while Crow's are, 'You didn't want to go because you'd started colouring in a picture of a dolphin you'd traced from the *National Geographic*, and your mum walked us there and when I fell and cut my knee you sat with me while everyone had a dance party in the garage and, when Gran came to get us, Ella's mum – I think her name was Natalie – gave us extra lamingtons for later.'

We have grown up to be pretty different, but with a past like that how can you grow apart?

'Do you think you'll recognise them?' Mum sounds worried. She's hardly touched her fancy salad. 'Your host family? Make sure you have their phone numbers.'

'I've got them. Everything's with my travel documents.' I feel suffocated, but also a bit comforted by my family's concerns. It's nice to be cared about.

'Moment of truth, Sof,' says Hana, placing her hands flat on the table. 'How will you be for money?'

Here is how much money I have saved: $2733. From babysitting and birthday money, and selling hand-drawn cards, bookmarks and prints at farmers markets and out of my schoolbag (I had the birthday card black market cornered at my school).

I knew right from the get-go that if I went on exchange, I had to be able to pay my way. We're not one of those families who can holiday every year. The times Dad doesn't have tutoring work at the uni, things are even tighter. He has a part-time job in a bookshop because he's a writer and a book critic who sometimes doesn't get enough freelance work. He'll teach a semester or two every now and then, but hates marking essays so he avoids it like salad in a burger. Anyway, all that means money isn't something we have lots of. While we've never gone hungry, we're not strangers to weeks of what's-in-the-pantry surprises and lots of mend-and-make-do clothes.

The past year has been a whirlwind of applications and passport forms – let's not even discuss how the passport photo turned out! Mum tried to reassure me that looking awful and suspicious is the whole point of passport photos. To pay for the passport I had to sell 61.5 cards – it actually hurt to hand over that money.

The plan is I can spend a maximum of twenty euros each day, but that's based on the idea that some days I won't spend any money at all. The host family is meant to feed you, so I figure it will be easy to live cheaply. I mean, what will my expenses be?

Museums. Metro. Maybe pencils. Definitely croissants.

'Don't worry about me,' I say. 'I'm all set.'

2

I can count the times I've been to the airport on one hand, and it's always been for other people. But now – now it's *my* turn. Excitement floods through me.

We park in the short-term parking and no-one grumbles about how much it's going to cost. I know they will on the way out, but at least I won't have to hear it. Because I am getting on a plane! Me!

'Remember we're parked in blue four,' says Mum. 'Who's going to remember where we are?'

'I will,' say Hana and Dad at the same time.

'I'll probably remember it wrong though,' adds Dad.

If I couldn't have a real backpacker's backpack, then I wish I at least had a suitcase I could carry in one hand: a hard, rectangular suitcase with a clunky handle, like from the olden days. I could swing it as I walked and place it down neatly next to me while I consulted a map. It would make for a much more romantic look. Like I'm in one of those Russian novels I've never read.

But instead I have this sensible suitcase on wheels that I'm borrowing from my grandfather. While I was packing,

I discovered $100 in one of the pockets, and when I tried to give it back to Pop, he just tapped the side of his nose and grinned. He has dementia so I'm not sure if he actually meant to give it to me, but Mum said just to keep it and remember to 'bloody send your grandfather a postcard once in a while!'

The airport is busy and I feel a bit lost, so I'm glad Dad comes with me to check in. 'Maybe they'll give you an upgrade.'

'Yeah, right,' I say. But while we wait for the queue to move, I imagine a first-class seat, probably next to someone famous, and a glass of champagne.

A woman at the check-in counter takes my passport.

'Any chance of an upgrade?' Dad asks, encouragingly.

The woman hardly looks up. 'Afraid not,' she says in a bored voice.

Dad and I shrug at each other, but I can't help feeling disappointed. Maybe a minor celebrity will sit next to me in economy.

The ticket lady gives me my boarding pass and my passport, and I pop them in my backpack pocket. My suitcase is weighed and tagged, and I watch over my shoulder as it disappears onto the conveyor belt. No going back now.

We find Mum and Hana near the gift shop, and I panic silently for a moment that I've dropped my passport, but it's still just in my backpack pocket where I put it.

At the point-of-no-return doors, my family insists on taking photos of me. I try not to make a face in every one of them, but it's hard. We are a family of face-makers in front of a camera.

'Keep your wits about you,' says Mum. 'Be careful over there.'

Everyone takes a turn to hug me, and I am surprised how tight I hold on.

Hana's smiling but she's crying too, her eyes all shimmery. 'Have a brilliant time,' she whispers into my ear. 'Throw yourself into all situations. Headfirst.'

'Thank you,' I say. I'm not sure how to thank her properly.

Then I am through the checkpoint and I am on my own. The combination of terror and absolute joy is unnerving.

I sit at one end of a bench of seats and tuck my backpack between my feet. I practise drawing aeroplanes in my sketchbook. It turns out I'm not so good at drawing aeroplanes. I can't seem to get the dimensions right.

I message Crow – to test whether she'll respond or not. She promised she would check messages and she even created an Instagram account. Crow is worried about internet privacy, but she reluctantly agreed to be online for me.

Crow replies half an hour later: *Haven't you left the country yet?*

There is a lot of time-killing when you're waiting for an international flight.

I decide to call Mum quickly.

'Hi, baby!' she says. 'We just got home. Are you through to the gate? How's it going?'

'Good,' I say. I'm unsure if I'm lying. The butterflies could be excitement.

'Have you looked up what movies you'll be able to

watch? Dad and I are just looking them up. Maybe we'll watch the same one as you!'

I feel both a sense of happy solace and a terrifying clutch of being left out. 'Don't watch anything new without me!' I'm about ready to burst into tears.

'Oh, Sof! Don't be a duffer.' Mum laugh-comforting me is only half comforting.

I just sit there, sneaking glances left and right to check if anyone can tell I'm being a big baby.

'I promise we won't watch anything new,' Mum says, her voice softer now. 'We'll just watch movies we've seen a dozen times before and, even then, only the ones you hate.'

I want to laugh, but I don't because I still feel sad.

'It seems unfair though,' she says. 'You're going to see so many new things. And Dad and I can't even go to the movies *once* while you're away?'

My flight is finally ready to board, and I can't believe the other passengers don't hear my heart beating as I show my boarding pass and passport, or feel the vibrations from my heart-thumps as I walk down the corridor to the plane.

Are all these people going to Paris? Where else might they be travelling? What are they going to do there? I wonder if I'll see any of them again.

There is the safety presentation and even though I've flown before (okay, yes, just once) I can't pull my eyes away from it. On this flight, the demonstration is presented as a funny little cartoon on our screens; no flight attendants in the aisles pointing this way and that while wearing inflatable vests. But cartoon comedy aside, I think: *I've got this – I'll be the first down the bouncy slide in my life vest with the light and whistle to attract attention.*

The plane pulls away from the gate. I can't believe it's going to be leaving the ground with me inside it. Can physics really be that tricksy?

As we take off, I can't stop thinking about air disasters. Debris floating on the ocean. What the heck is with all this doom and gloom? Who am I? Crow?

I try to think light thoughts. Cotton wool. Bubbles. Feathers. Soufflé.

If we fly safely all the way to Paris, I am going to go to a café with cane chairs and a green striped awning and I am going to eat a soufflé.

I sketch croissants on my knee with my fingertip. I sketch a baker's dozen. I cross the fingers of my left hand for luck.

I decide that I love the plane when it is dark; it makes me laugh to think of the flight attendants just being all *okay, bedtime, night-night everyone.* I love all the whispering, and it's fun to glance down the rows as I walk back from the bathroom to see which films everyone has chosen.

I keep my little overhead light on and doodle my dreams and plans. I copy the flight path into my notepad – dotted lines and freehand arcs. Tiny aeroplane sketches, approximations of countries and continents, oceans and seas that I always get wrong when we do the quiz in the newspaper. I am going so far away. 16,760 kilometres, or thereabouts.

I am all alone in the world.

In my exchange application, I highlighted my sense of adventure and my resilience. Hana helped with that part and reassured me that even if some of my strengths weren't technically accurate, it's what they would want to hear. She said, 'I'm sure that when you're older these things might be true from time to time.'

I wrote about how much I love art and philosophy and how I've been wanting to visit France ever since I could remember, and I swear all of this came straight from my heart.

I've been really lucky already – between the exchange organisation and my host family, I've got a place in a high school, a *lycée*, for the Arts. Because of this, it might be possible to lay the foundation for going back to do Art in Paris for university. It seems like a very amorphous thing, but I popped it in my dream world. It fit there very nicely.

I wake up to my ears popping as the plane makes its descent, and I press my face to the window for my first glimpse. My eyes dart across the expanse of the big old city. Is that the Eiffel Tower? Maybe!

The flight attendant welcomes us in French. '*Mesdames et messieurs, bienvenue à Paris Charles de Gaulle.*' The local time is 3.45 pm, and the temperature a cool two degrees Celsius.

Walking down the aisle, towards the exit, I start to feel giddy with anticipation. I climbed into a metal tube and, by physics and magic, have been catapulted across the world. I have flown across oceans and lands and places I've never been (because I've never been anywhere except for Wilsons Prom on family holidays, and to Sydney once).

I turn a corner and here I am.

In France.

Bienvenue.

3

Claudette and Léon are waiting between the gate and the baggage carousel, where we'd organised. And looking exactly like their photo: she is tall and slim, with sleek brown hair, shoulder length and just so. She wears a rust-coloured coat and her long, thin legs are anchored to the ground by a pair of neat boots. Léon is wearing a tailored winter coat and a short woollen scarf looped and knotted around his neck. He looks confident and has ruddy cheeks like an illustration of a farmer in a children's storybook.

They recognise me, even though they've only seen a photo of a girl who has never left home. A girl in a floral blouse with a denim dress over the top. A girl with an at-home haircut, newly bobbed. That girl must look like such a child.

'*Bonjour, Sofie!*' they say, smiling. '*Bienvenue en France!*'

'*Bonjour*,' I say, and my voice is a squeak. I feel shy and somehow all the French words have escaped me, from *bonjour* onwards. The bags begin to travel around the carousel, and people push and jostle to be first.

The exchange organisation allocates you to a family that shares your interests, so I have been placed with the Durant family. Two parents, one child (around my age). Léon is an artist, Claudette works for a gallery, and their daughter, Delphine, goes to a prestigious music high school. We'd spoken once on the phone and they'd emailed me too, saying that they would be pleased to welcome me into their home. 'And we speak a little English, too,' they promised. They would introduce me to France, French culture, French food, French customs.

I looked up Léon Durant online back when we were first assigned to each other: he's had a number of exhibitions in Paris, in Bordeaux and even in Berlin. The internet calls his work Post-Expressionism but also Dada, and I'm still learning art styles and art history so I can't confirm or deny the internet's truth. The works I found online were full of deep colour and strange, unsettling faces, and made me intrigued by the person who created them.

I imagine a garret apartment filled with heavy, old-fashioned furniture (passed down the generations) and thick Turkish rugs and red wine and paintings and a host of arty, sophisticated friends.

'We can speak English with you tonight,' says Claudette, her words cautious but fluent.

'But French from tomorrow!' says Léon. He's tall and a bit plump, and his accent in English is thick and clichéd. I like him right away.

'Okay!' I say. Tomorrow my words will have returned, I'm fairly confident. I see my bag appear, the hot pink ribbon that Hana tied to its handle screaming frilly neon. I scoot over to grab it, feeling a mix of out of place, excited and grimy.

'Now. It is very cold today, so it is good you have this coat.' Claudette points to my jacket, which I'm clutching under my arm.

I quickly put the coat on and grip the handle of my grandfather's suitcase. I follow close behind Claudette and Léon and I try to anticipate the weather. Through the doors is a grey footpath, a grey road, and the doors are opening and … it's like putting my face in the freezer.

A wind whips around and actually takes my breath with it for a moment, with an audible *whoosh*.

Claudette and Léon laugh, which makes me laugh too, in spite of being horrified.

Where have I arrived? It is like another world. It's only a five-minute walk through the car park but I take that time to rethink my every action.

My case hardly fits inside their tiny car and completely fills the boot (what's the word for boot in French?). We all pile in like popes in a Volkswagen, and drive on the wrong side of the road, winding around and around, until we eventually pop out of the maze of the airport. Both of them grumble about the cost of parking, which makes me feel a smidge more at home.

Claudette is driving, and Léon has his phone in his hand. They speak to each other in fast French, and I feel bulky in my coat. They seem cross or exasperated by something.

I watch suburbs and concrete freeway barriers pass by the window, mesmerised and just a little bewildered. So far, France is cold but it isn't very interesting. Or, at least, it isn't very French.

Bare trees stretch their scraggly arms into the white smudgy sky. I sketch them on my knee.

'I'm sorry, Sofie.' Claudette speaks over her shoulder. I can see a fine silver earring dangling from her ear. 'Our daughter, Delphine, is telling us she will be out tonight.'

I wonder if Delphine is out in a café, smoking cigarettes and discussing *philosophie*. In our French textbooks the teenagers go to *le jardin zoologique* and *la fête de la musique*. Maybe Delphine is doing that, or perhaps she's at a dance party. Maybe she'll invite me along to dance parties – not something I've done much of, if I'm honest, but I'm here to broaden my experiences and my mind, so why not?

'Yes, we asked her to be home to meet you, but—' Léon shrugs a what-can-you-do kind of shrug. 'She is going to a piano concert after her running training. Our daughter, she is very dedicated.'

A piano-playing athlete. I'm intrigued.

After about half an hour, Claudette pulls the car off the freeway – I flinch as we turn the 'wrong way' into one street after another. I feel quite lucky that I can't drive yet, and so won't have to.

I will have to be careful when I cross the road though.

'This is Belleville, our *quartier* of Paris,' explains Léon. The way he pronounces *quartier*, the word for neighbourhood, like *Cartier*, like the jewellery.

'Oh,' I say. Belleville is … not quite how I imagined Paris. It is certainly not the Cartier in the jewellery box of this city.

There are no wrought-iron balconies. No window

boxes with colourful flowers (to be fair, it *is* the middle of winter), and all the buildings are grey and dingy and plain. They're modern, boxy, grubby, like the commission flats back home. There's rubbish on the footpaths, in piles.

We pull up outside one of the grey-brown buildings, and Léon parallel parks in between two cars that look very much like theirs. They help me pull my suitcase towards a very secure-looking gate, and Léon punches in a long code to open it.

When I step into the flat, I feel the dream move another step away. I try to hold onto it as they show me around. I take in everything: the furniture, the décor, the art on the walls. Everything is clean and nice … it's all just a bit plain. Pale wood and sleek modern chairs, tables, low grey sofa. It reminds me of … it's all very Ikea showroom, if I'm being honest.

There's a pile of sheet music on a side table – classical, from what I know of music – and I imagine going along to one of Delphine's piano concerts.

Claudette and Léon show me where the *mot de passe* for the wifi is written down in idiosyncratic French handwriting, on a Post-it note underneath the computer keyboard. I connect and excuse myself to type out a 'we've arrived, everything is fine (everything is not exactly as I'd imagined)' message to my family.

There is some art on the walls, though, and I wonder which pieces are Léon's.

'Do you paint at the apartment?' I ask.

'No, no, no.' He waves a hand and I'm reminded of

my sister's gesturing. 'I have an atelier in the fifth. That is where I work.'

An atelier! What a dream! I hope he'll let me look around it while I'm here; I have an instant daydream of setting up in a corner as Léon guides my painting and gives me tips, us working together with light streaming in the windows. I already feel like I'll create wonderful art in Léon's atelier.

There is that buzz of excitement I'd been feeling for weeks, for a year, since Hana first raised this whole thing as a possibility. Never mind the Ikea bookcase – *I'm in Paris!*

I long to go for a walk and let this buzzing circulate, but it is already well and truly dark outside. It's probably not the done thing to go walking at night in a city you've only just arrived in. It would probably reflect badly on Léon and Claudette if I got lost or stolen on my first night.

I am in Paris and I cannot get to sleep.

I lie in bed and I am excited and scared and exhausted and pumping with adrenaline. *I am in Paris I am in Paris I am in Paris.*

I wonder if I should get back up again and unpack. Claudette had indicated each drawer in turn as she showed me where I could put my things, and she pushed across some coats already hanging in the cupboard to make room.

I already knew that a drawer is *un tiroir* but had to learn that a coat hanger is *un cintre* (it will be a challenge to get my tongue around that sound … *cintre cintre cintre*). And I was delighted that French people truly say *bonne nuit* at night-time.

I feel like I will never go to sleep. I look out the window

for a while, but all I can see is the dark of the night, the grey concrete of the building next door in the shimmer of a yellow street light. I imagine painting the light in thick oil paints.

The word for car boot in French is *le coffre*.

Boots that you wear on your feet are *les bottes*.

I wonder when Delphine will come home. I half listen for the front door or for footsteps along the hall, as I sit in bed with my sketchbook on my knee.

… then the next thing I know my alarm is trilling a *wake up wake up* tune, and I am still sitting up in bed with my sketchbook only just slipped from my hands. I can't believe I fell asleep like passing out. Like I died momentarily and then was revived.

Lucky I was using a pencil. Imagine if I'd ink-stained the Durants' sheets on my first night.

I don't think I dreamed. Or if I did, I dreamed about lying awake in this tiny room and all the funny smells. The funny smells aren't bad ones: a laundry detergent I've never smelled before; coffee wafting from the kitchen; my own body taken out of context.

I get dressed right away, shoving my pjs under the pillow and pulling up the doona roughly, so the bed looks made (I hardly ever do this at home). Jeans, long-sleeve top, jumper, my wombat brooch for luck.

I feel strangely anxious about leaving the bedroom that will be my bedroom for the next five months, but I have a talk with myself and run through the morning-time vocab I've practised so many times in class:

Bonjour. Hello.

Tu as bien dormi? Did you sleep well?

Oui, merci. Yes, thank you.

Pour le petit déjeuner, je prends un croissant, un chocolat chaud et un jus d'orange. For breakfast I have a croissant, hot chocolate and orange juice.

The crappy illustrations in our French textbooks always made us laugh – the funny cartoon people enjoying their very French breakfast.

I walk down the hallway that will be my hallway for five months, into the kitchen that will be my kitchen for five months, following the low voices and morning sounds of bowls sliding onto the table and cutlery clinking that will be my sounds for the next five months. How bizarre is it to be on the other side of the world?

'*Bonjour, Sofie,*' says Claudette.

'*Tu as bien dormi?*' asks Léon.

'*Oui, merci,*' I say, and my voice is very small. It must be hungry, this little voice. I am sure I am braver than this.

'*Tu bois du café?*' Claudette asks.

I pause. I consider faking it, pretending that I drink coffee all the time. Then, '*Non, pas souvent,*' I admit. 'Errr. *Non, merci.*'

'*Un chocolat chaud?*'

I can't believe this moment has walked out of the textbook, out of the daydream, and into reality. Hot chocolate for breakfast? I mean, YES PLEASE.

'*Oui, s'il te plaît.*'

In front of me is a baguette. I watch Léon, who uses his hands to break off a piece, gouges it into two with his thumbs, then picks up his knife to greedily smear butter and jam onto each wodge of baguette.

'*Tartine?*' he says through a mouthful, as he pushes the baguette towards me.

I copy his actions. As I am spreading the butter from an oval-shaped plastic container with the word *Président* on it, Claudette places a bowl in front of me. Ikea. We have the same at home. They are my favourite cornflakes bowls. It makes me smile. Then she pours hot chocolate from a saucepan into the bowl – what seems like litres of it.

I have to pick it up with both hands. As I blow on the top of the hot chocolate to cool it, I look around the kitchen – *how absolutely strange to think I am going to live here for five months!* There are mugs hanging on little hooks, a rack of spices on the wall, big pots and saucepans on a shelf, and floral wallpaper that seems very unlike Claudette and Léon (not that I know them well at all yet).

I drink and play it cool. It is absolutely delicious, the hot chocolate. But also this new life.

For breakfast I eat a *tartine* with jam and drink a giant hot chocolate. This is exactly what I'd wanted. I know it's just breakfast. But it's what the breakfast represents: a dream, a lot of work, and a lot of luck. How lucky am I? Even as I am thinking it, I know I'm being silly, and at the same time I feel very strange in an anticipatory kind of way. But mostly I feel like dancing with joy.

'*Elle est où, Delphine?*' I ask. (I'd practised this too.) Where is Delphine?

Claudette sips her coffee and speaks to me in slow, clear French. 'Delphine's gone to school already – she has running training before classes start. Do you enjoy running?'

Crow and I would have snorted with laughter if we'd been together and heard this question. But now I fold my hands politely in my lap (I keep feeling the urge to be very small and not take up much room). '*Un peu*,' I say. A bit. 'I walk a lot, at home in Melbourne.'

Smiles all around. I'm speaking French! We are so polite! We strangers who now live together.

After breakfast, I need to hotfoot it to meet the exchange coordinator.

'Are you ready, Sofie? I'll accompany you on the *métro*.'

Claudette is going to come with me on the metro, yes, I understood that. I feel relieved because I know I'll be lost as soon as I step outside.

I run to my bedroom and grab my bag, making sure I have some cash. I fan out my euros. There are a lot here for now – enough, I hope. I put a twenty euro note in my purse and stash the rest.

Back in the kitchen, I throw my backpack on and squash a beanie on my head.

'Okay,' says Claudette. 'Let's go!'

Claudette helps me buy a travel card, and we pick up a map of all the metro lines, and then I follow her down to the platform.

There are funny little handles on the metro doors – they look a bit like the window winders in Mum's ancient car. I watch people come in and out so I'll know how to use them when the time comes.

We travel from Belleville on the blue 2 line, through the stops Colonel Fabien, Jaurès, Stalingrad, La Chapelle, Barbès–Rochechouart (I practise saying this, because it's tongue-twisty: *bar-bess rosh-esh-shwar*), Anvers, Pigalle, Blanche, Place de Clichy, Rome, Villiers, Monceau, Courcelles, Ternes. So many places to explore.

At the metro stop Charles de Gaulle–Étoile – named for both General Charles de Gaulle, President of France in the 1960s, and also l'Étoile, the roundabout that the Arc de Triomphe sits upon – Claudette pushes me gently towards the doors and says, '*À ce soir!*'

And then I am off the train, and the train is leaving with Claudette on it, and I am on the platform and on my own. On my own IN PARIS.

I find the exit and climb up to street level, feeling hot in my new-old coat borrowed from Mum. But when I get out and am slammed with an icy wind, I'm so grateful for it. And for my scarf. I pull my sleeves over my hands and shove my hands in my pockets. I remember I need to be aware of pickpockets, though I try not to look too worried so I won't be an easy target. The guidebooks all say to take care on the metro. So far, I still have all my stuff.

Then, I forget all about pickpockets and icy blasts because – there it is.

L'Arc de Triomphe.

The real true Arc de Triomphe, in its grey-beige stone iconic beauty. I am seeing it with my own two eyes and my own one heart is leaping.

Paris, Paris, Paris, Paris!

5

Cars hurtle dangerously around l'Étoile. I've read that they do this – it was in our school textbook. There are twelve roads that all converge at the massive roundabout, giving it a star shape if viewed from above (perhaps from the top of the Arc de Triomphe, which is *right before my eyes!*) – which is how it got its name.

But how to get across? For a moment I consider dashing through traffic, but I don't want to die today. It turns out you have to go underneath the road. I scurry down the stairs, past the signs I'd missed at first, along the passage, and then up up up again.

We were given instructions in our orientation booklet. I'm looking for Toby, the coordinator, and I spot him among a group of people who kind of look my age. I can tell it's Toby on account of him clearly being an adult. An adult wearing a tweed cap, standing in the middle of a group of teenagers. He is also holding a big red umbrella, folded up.

Bonjour or hello? I wonder. I decide to wave.

'Hello!' says Toby, in English. In fact he has an English

accent. This is not what I expected. The information pack said our exchange coordinator would speak English, but I had imagined him differently (with a French accent and whatnot).

'Hi. I'm Sofie.'

He looks down at his list. 'Excellent – one of our Australians. It's nice to meet you.' Then three more new people show up and he ticks them off his list too.

There are about thirty of us students altogether, and I know from the orientation booklet that we come from twelve different countries and between us speak nine different languages. French is supposed to be our common tongue, though there's a lot of English flying around, thank goodness.

Before leaving Australia, I thought I'd developed a pretty good command of French. But now I am feeling much less sure of myself and much more tongue-tied. Vocabulary just tumbles out of my head.

Toby gathers us and waves us through the underpass and back up to the wide boulevard that is the Avenue des Champs-Élysées.

I am about to walk down the Champs-Élysées.

And so begins my first real walk in Paris.

Even in the cold, even with the trees all bare, even as part of a giant group led by a man holding a red umbrella above his head, I feel dizzy with dreams coming true.

'Hi,' a girl's voice says, pulling me out of my dream. I hadn't noticed her standing next to me. She has long black hair and an Australian accent. 'I'm Rupa.'

'I'm Sofie,' I reply, holding out my hand, which she

awkwardly shakes.

'You'll notice that most people "*faire la bise*" here,' says Toby, looming over us. 'Get used to being closer to strangers than you normally would. Right cheek, then left cheek.' He mimes giving air kisses. *Mwah mwah.*

It's even more awkward now, as we look at each other. Is he expecting us to re-greet each other? I feel myself blush. It had been an automatic action to extend my hand – Hana had drilled me on shaking hands to be polite, but she clearly failed to factor in *les bises.*

'We're good,' says Rupa in a dry tone. The expression on her face is so funny that we both burst out laughing.

Toby smiles goofily and moves away, calling out, '*Allons-y!* Let's go!'

We set off as a group. For a moment I wish I was setting out to explore by myself. It feels rude that all of these people are in *my* city as I am introducing myself to it. But Rupa seems nice and she is gazing around with an appropriate amount of wonder.

'I love how wide these footpaths are,' I say aloud. The footpaths are flat concrete blocks, and they're so wide – metres and metres between the shops and the road.

Rupa reaches out her hand. 'Want me to take a photo of you?'

'Sure.' I pass her my phone and stand at the edge of the footpath, staring down the wide, wide boulevard. 'Thanks,' I say as she gives me back my phone. 'This will be perfect to send home to my parents.'

For my Insta feed I focus on the smaller details. Cobbles. A shopfront with a wooden board across its window. Video, photo, boomerang of cars driving past.

Renoir or Monet, or even Coco Chanel probably walked down this very street at least once, just as I am walking down it now.

'It's interesting to think about how much damage the *gilets jaunes* did to this place,' says Toby to the group. 'And how even now you can't really tell.'

'What's *gilets jaunes*?' I ask in English.

'The yellow vests?' says an American guy in a black puffer jacket, in a prompting kind of tone.

'Oh yes!' I try to be quick to cover my ignorance. Crow had talked *at length* about the yellow vests. It had been on the news at home a lot in the last month or so, since the first explosive protests in November. I know that it all started over the proposed increase of petrol prices and quickly grew to protests all across the country.

'Is it just me or do all the world's problems seem to start over petrol and oil?' I say out loud.

The guy nods. 'Yeah, pretty much.'

'I'm a bit confused,' Crow had said. 'I can't tell if the protesters are left-wing or right-wing. It seems like they're both.' Whatever their political leaning, they all wear yellow hi-vis jackets for a uniform, and they've been blockading freeways, villages, and Parisian streets. 'Setting shit on fire,' Crow said. (Fire is Crow's not-so-secret fascination. Not that she's a pyromaniac or anything. But 'Burn it down!' is usually what she says when anything is going wrong.)

Toby's voice booms over my thoughts. 'The lights are still up from Christmas, so if you come down after dark you'll see something really pretty.'

I look up at the strings of lights, unlit for now, and find I much prefer thinking about Christmas lights than people in yellow vests kicking in windows.

We walk to the Louvre, but we don't go in. 'You'll all get a chance to visit while you're here,' says Toby. 'Today is just an introduction to the city.'

But there goes my heart again, jumping at the sight of those iconic glass pyramids.

'I've been here already,' a red-headed girl with an English accent says to me. 'On holidays with my family. But it was so big we couldn't see it all. Do you like art?'

I can't formulate words to express the scope of my love for art. About getting lost in something beautiful, made by someone who has thought about beauty and wonder, whether it be in paint or pencil or clay. How I can stare at brushstrokes and colour and line for hours, and the shiver it sends through me. How it makes me feel like everything is as it should be.

So I just say, 'Yes, yes I do.'

Toby tells us about how during World War II the French took the art out of the museums and moved it to places it would be safe. I guess I haven't thought about art in times of war very much.

We walk across a bridge, le Pont Notre Dame, and then there is another icon: the cathedral. I am not from a churchy family, but I have thought almost religiously about Paris, and the Notre Dame is one of the things that embodies the city for me.

I am desperate to walk around the back, where I know from photos that the building is extra-interesting with its flying buttresses (I think it was the term 'flying buttresses' that first took my fancy), but Toby herds us across the next bridge and onto the Left Bank. *It's okay*, I think. *I'll come back. I've got time.*

Things I already know about the Left Bank:

1. In French you say *rive gauche.*
2. It's where all the artists and writers have hung out through history.
3. It's a site of bohemian Paris.

'Over there is Shakespeare and Company,' says Toby, pointing. 'It's maybe the most famous English-language bookshop in the city. Worth a visit.'

I already know about Shakespeare and Company, so I feel pretty smug.

'They published *Ulysses* by James Joyce,' says the red-haired girl, and her tone brings my previous smugness down a notch. Now I am thinking, *Who cares who knows what?*

'Have you read it?' I ask.

'Not yet. But I will,' she says and pushes ahead of me.

We wind through some narrow, busy streets in the Latin Quarter, where Toby points out all the places to get food and explains about *la formule* – a meal plan that might include a drink, a panini and a dessert. The places are tiny hole-in-the-wall sandwich and kebab restaurants, where you can sit at one of two or three small tables inside or order takeaway through a big window counter. I choose a cheese and tomato panini, and a drink. It's a cheaper option than the one with dessert so I save one euro and fifty cents.

We follow Toby across a large intersection to eat our lunch on the freezing banks of the Seine.

'It's actually not so cold at the moment,' says Toby. 'We might have snow in the coming weeks though.'

Snow! My teeth chatter as I drink a *Coca-light*.

After lunch we continue along the river and visit the exchange program's office in the 7th arrondissement. The roads are wider here and it feels more modern, in spite of the iconic Haussmann buildings.

Toby reminds us about the rules for the exchange. 'Attend school,' he says. 'That's why you're here. Keep curfew. Don't break laws. Keep away from the *gilets jaunes*. Check in with your coordinator – that's me. Engage with the culture and especially the language. Don't drink alcohol.'

I hadn't thought about alcohol. I will definitely be trying wine if it's offered. Preferably served by the woman in Manet's *A Bar at the Folies-Bergère*.

There is a large world map on one of the walls with pins and a basket of string, and Toby encourages us to mark our path in getting here. I wind a green string around the pin sitting in Melbourne (it's quite fat with string already) and I stretch it in a straight line to Dubai (but is it the same line as my flight path?), where I wind it just once, before stretching it again to Paris and hooking it to the big peg that anchors all our lines in place.

'Do you like your host family?' I ask the guy standing by me. It's the American puffer jacket guy from earlier.

Dan, I think he said his name was.

He shakes his head. 'I haven't met them. We're still at the hostel. But I get the train tomorrow and they're going to pick me up. I think it's four hours away or something.'

'Oh! I'm staying in Paris.' I hadn't really thought about the students not based in Paris. 'What's the town you're staying in called?'

'Um, I think it's Sou-il-lack or something. I can't actually pronounce it. Not a very good sign, probably. It's in the southwest region.'

He is *nervous*! I feel braver thanks to his nerves. Is that terrible? But I've already survived my first night with my host family and they seem happy to have me. I try not to think about Delphine, my host sister, who I haven't met yet and am already intimidated by.

I'm not sure if the floaty, dazed feeling in me is jet lag or if I am Paris-drunk.

To end the day's tour, we walk along the Seine, and as the Eiffel Tower comes into view, I am suddenly *present* again. The feel of the footpath under my feet is, literally and comfortingly, grounding.

Some of the group are complaining about how sore their feet are, that they are cold, that they'd walked further today than ever before.

I have always been a wanderer. When I was a toddler I wandered off and ended up in a duck pond at the Botanical Gardens. It was fortunate I didn't drown, especially since my sister just stood and shouted for our parents instead of dragging me out.

I wander now, still. Sometimes it frustrates my parents. They say, 'But where do you go?' and I just say, 'Oh, here and there.' I get lost a lot, but I always find my way back eventually.

My heart leaps again and again as I walk along the Seine, the Eiffel Tower just eiffeling away. *This* is exactly what I had been hoping for! I lag behind the group and rewind my scarf.

The stone buildings cry out for me to touch them. To run my hand across their smooth surfaces and fall into history through them.

I feel a nudge at my elbow. Dan is grinning across at me, the delight on his face surely mirroring my own, and he says, 'I can't believe we're here.'

I hadn't needed to worry about the metro door handles. I get off the train successfully – *clu-clunk* goes the funny little handle as I twist it up.

As I step out of the metro at Belleville and start the walk back to the apartment, I have a sudden and strange flash: *This is where I live.* I suppose I've been concentrating so much on getting back without getting lost that I haven't been thinking about the bigger picture.

In Belleville there is graffiti everywhere, and run-down shops and pawnbrokers. Most things look a bit grimy – and there is a rotten smell. I vaguely remember Claudette saying something last night about an open-air market (*marché* being one of the easiest French words to remember thanks to years of Mum, Dad and Hana pretending to be posh: 'Just popping out to the *supermarché*!'). The streets are strewn with rubbish – food scraps and cardboard and drink cans are everywhere. I feel as though reality is smacking me in the face, and I don't like it.

This is not what I expected.

It's not often that I can't disappear into my dreamscape,

but now is one of those times – even after the day I've had. I grit my teeth and try to recapture the feeling of standing beneath the Eiffel Tower.

I remember all the 'left then right then right agains' and arrive back at the flat without any navigational problems, but with heavy feet and jet-lagged confusion.

I enter the code on the gate and then the second code at the door. I stare at the two elevators in the lobby because a little voice inside me is saying, *What had Claudette explained about the lifts?* One stops at all the odd-numbered floors and one at all the even-numbered. What even is this, France?

By chance more than good memory, I enter the correct one and go up in a lift that clangs. The Durants' flat is number forty-four on the fourth floor. I like the symmetry and neatness of the numbers.

Because I don't have a key yet, I knock on the door and hope someone is home. Claudette and Léon had promised one of them would be there by 5 pm – and it's 5.45 pm now – but I don't know yet if they are people of their word.

The door is opened by a stranger. Have I knocked on the right door? Dread runs through me. But no, there is the '44' on the door.

It's a girl – tall and slender, in jeans and a soft woollen jumper and sock feet – and I'm nearly sure I know who she is. Her face is similar to Claudette's, but not quite.

'*Bonjour?*' I say, and touch my hand to my chest. '*Sofie?*' It comes out like I'm not sure of my own identity.

The girl smiles. '*Bien sûr.* Of course.'

I realise that this is the mystery daughter of Léon and Claudette – the elusive Delphine – despite the fact that she doesn't look like a teenager, or any teenagers I've known in real life. In the photo the Durants emailed through, Delphine's hair was shorter and her face rounder, but between then and now her face has changed. She looks older, and her hair hangs shiny and soft to her waist.

She moves back and I step inside. There's a space (as I was shown yesterday) to put outdoor shoes and hang coats, and I do these things and try to think of how to begin a conversation with this new stranger.

Delphine at first glance (and second glance) is stunningly beautiful, with her long dark brown hair and a way of moving that makes it look like each muscle of her body is engaged at all times. I know from the emails exchanged with her parents that we are about the same age, but now I'm seeing her in real life, Delphine is a grown-up. She is sophisticated and put together, prim and proper. I feel like the opposite of all those things, and I am intimidated all over again.

'It's nice to meet you, Sofie,' she says in English. Her voice is rich and mature. She leans in and kisses me on one cheek – *mwah* – and the other – *mwah* – and I can feel my face going a bit pink. 'My parents are late at work.'

'Okay,' is all I say.

So this is my host family. It feels very strange to have a new family all of a sudden.

'So why did you decide to come to France?' asks Delphine, in English. She takes a Tupperware container out of the fridge, opens it and sniffs the contents.

Trying to explain about art and dreams and the quest for

beauty and the shape of leaves, gumnuts and cracks turns out to be really hard. So I just simplify things. 'I like the language. And it is a good opportunity.'

She scoops rice salad from the container into a bowl. Takes some roast chicken from another container and places a piece on each of the two plates she has laid on the table. 'I did an exchange to England.'

'Oh, yes?' I say. 'Did you enjoy it?'

'I did. It really helped my English. I was in York last year. It's still strange being back.'

She places half a baguette on the table and sits down behind one of the plates. '*Bon appétit.*'

I sit and follow Delphine's lead, taking a spoonful of rice salad, breaking off a chunk of baguette with my hands.

Claudette is apologetic when she arrives back at the house. 'I'm sorry I am late, Sofie,' she says in French. 'I had a reunion. Next time I will send you a message.'

I nod, and smile to show I don't mind, and wonder what kind of reunion she had been at. When my mum went to her high school reunion she had (allegedly) 'just one too many wines' and (fact) went dancing until 2 am.

'*Réunion* means meeting,' Delphine explains, like she can see into my brain.

Claudette puts her coat away in the hall cupboard and boils the kettle. Delphine brings out a selection of cheeses from the fridge, and I watch as she cuts slivers of each type and places them on her dinner plate – no separate cheese plate – and slowly eats them with bits of bread left over from her dinner.

I copy her, though I am fearful of the wedge of blue, crumbly and mouldy, so I choose not to try it.

Claudette makes herself a tea and sits with us.

'In Australia,' I say, 'we eat cheese before dinner – with drinks.' Delphine puts the lid back on the cheeses and returns them to the fridge. I don't add that at barbeques and dinner parties it's unlikely there would be any cheese left over – I've watched my parents' friends polish off a supermarket brie within minutes. I imagine the cheeses I'm eating now come from a cheese shop though.

It is now 9.30 pm. *Is it too early for bed?* I wonder. I decide no, it isn't, and say, 'I'm just going to get ready for tomorrow. School.'

'*Bonne nuit, Sofie.*'

Before leaving the kitchen, I stop myself and turn back. 'Should I …?' I point at the dishes and make a scrubbing motion.

'I will put everything in the dishwasher,' says Claudette.

In my room, as I gather my things together, I feel outside of myself. I feel excited and happy and disappointed, all at the one time. I'm out of place, but I can't quite bring myself to admit it. I have worked so hard to be here.

This outside-of-myself, dreamy, jet-lagged, displaced feeling is probably what makes all of my stuff take on talismanic qualities. I open the suitcase and bring out my things – each one sparking joy and comfort – and I give them homes in my new room.

I have never kept a journal, but I don't want to forget my days here. I have a blank notebook, and so on my second night in Paris after my first real day, I start.

Except a whole bank page seems overwhelming when the idea is to fill it with words. Instead, I draw a funny little map, like a mind map, of the places we walked. I draw the red-haired girl leaning against the glass pyramid of the Louvre while reading James Joyce. I draw landmarks, and it's easier to write labels alongside. I note the time it took to walk between particular sounds and smells.

Today I walked along the Seine river. I stood in front of the Notre Dame, and I looked up and saw the gargoyles with my own eyes. I stood before the Eiffel Tower. How can this be? Are we *allowed* to get everything we've ever wanted?

This is everything I expected.

My head feels light and confused, and my body is heavy, so I lie down on the bed without even changing into my pyjamas. There's a siren outside – even the sirens are different.

This is not what I expected.

Décalage horaire. Jet lag.

7

Sofie

It suddenly seems very rude that
I have to go to school when I'm
meant to be on summer holidays.

Crow

Yep that really sucks for you.

And how are you filling your
endless days of freedom?

You know. Sex, drugs, rock'n'roll.

So sleeping the morning away and
then hanging out with your gran?

Pretty much.

– Overnight chats with Crow

I go with Léon on my first day at school. I'm pretty sure he'd explained that he would come with me and then go to his studio for the day. I still feel like I'm listening underwater though, and only picking up snippets of conversations. Getting over jet lag is like having a bad flu – like I'm weak and dragging my whole weight around.

I layer up before leaving – my plans for being chic and put together set aside in exchange for being warm. I feel like a genius for putting on a pair of tights underneath my jeans.

I'd combed all my local op shops for new outfits after I found out I was going to France. It felt important to have a new look for my exchange. Hana never cared about clothes, so I think I went the opposite way. I love beautiful things, so I try to wear clothes that feel nice and look pretty. In the past I have favoured floaty dresses, with lots of colours and patterns. 'Librarian chic', Mum sometimes called my style. To get ready for France, I made a few alterations to my look. The first one was chopping a fringe in, which was a terrible mistake. It ended up shorter than I intended and revealed a cowlick that sent part of my fringe skew-whiff. At least it would grow out.

In Paris, my style was going to be simple and structured. I chose dark jeans and oversized tops that I could layer. I found shapeless black dresses I could cinch in with statement belts. Skivvies to wear underneath. Fewer colours, a capsule wardrobe, long beaded necklaces and scarves for pops of colour.

Crow made fun of me for 'preparing a uniform', as she called it. 'Nice reinvention,' she teased. 'Have you got your stripy top and your jaunty beret ready too? Your Chanel perfume?' (Why yes, I spritzed some Chanel onto bits of cardboard in Myer and tucked them into my suitcase in the hope it'd infuse my clothes. So?)

'Shut up,' I'd said, ineloquently.

The school is a squat concrete block, like the rest of the buildings in the *quartier.* I look for graffiti in the hope of some colour or personality, like the streets around the metro stop, but everything I see here is ugly and dull. Black spray paint scrawls across the wall, making words I can't understand.

I had imagined a *lycée* dedicated to the Arts would be a bit more interesting. Even inside the building is shabbier than I'd expected. But it has that smell of school, so I guess that's a comfort in some ways.

In the principal's office Léon talks fast and gruffly, and the principal – *la directrice* – is businesslike, and neither of them really pay me much attention. She gives me my class schedule and my ID card. 'You must show this to get in and out of the school, and for taking your lunch also.'

I nod.

'I understand that you are interested in plastic art,' she continues.

Léon nods.

'Plastic art?' I ask. *Plastic art?! I want to draw. Not work with plastic. I'm ANTI-plastic.*

Turns out *Arts Plastiques* is the French way of saying Fine Arts. Which, yes, is what I want to do. I want to study Fine Arts and I want to be an artist.

'Véronique said your drawing was strong,' says Léon. Véronique is the art teacher here at the *lycée*, and I knew from our emails that Léon used to teach at this school before he began tutoring at the university. 'And she thought you would enjoy some more focused study of artistic practices. This particular course is for *lycée* students who plan to attend the *grandes écoles* for art.'

The *grandes écoles* are universities that specialise in particular courses and that are really, really hard to get into. They're kind of like the Ivy League colleges of France. I know about the École Nationale Supérieure des Beaux-Arts – the Fine Arts Academy. This is more than I could have ever dreamed!

I must be smiling excessively because both Léon and the *directrice* are smiling back at me in a slightly condescending way, but I don't even care.

'Okay, Sofie. *À ce soir. Tu as la clé?*' asks Léon. See you tonight. You have the key?

The interview bit is over and they are standing up. I jump to my feet as Léon salute-waves and leaves the room.

I suddenly need to double-check that I do have the key. I feel for it down the bottom of my tote and hold onto it while the *directrice* walks me to class.

I feel a normal amount of nervousness in the face of meeting so many strangers. When we go into the classroom, I can only scan the room, hardly focusing on the faces.

'I present you Sofie, who has come all the way from Australia.' Then, with a smile and a jangle of her bracelets, the *directrice* is away – *bonne journée* – and I'm pointed towards an empty seat next to a boy with neat lightning bolts shaved into his hair, who nods at me.

The French word for someone who has come from another country is *étranger*. Stranger. *I* am the stranger. And that makes me feel a bit more confident in a way. Strangers are mysterious.

I'm not sure if I am supposed to understand what is going on, and I can't remember how the grades I get during my exchange are counted when I get home. Right now it seems very unfair to be marked when my classes are all in another language!

I let the words and the sounds wash over me, and open my notebook when everyone else opens theirs. Nobody has a laptop, which makes me glad I didn't bring mine along.

I watch the teacher, Madame Michel. Not to understand the class – I decided after five minutes that there is no point. Everyone speaks so fast! The language is just scooting by my poor jet-lagged ears. But I look at her fashion. I love the woollen scarf she has draped around her neck, the thin white blouse and the crisp navy blue trousers. She isn't wearing any jewellery. I draw myself in her outfit to see how I might look, taking notes and inspiration from her.

A couple of girls from my class ask me to come with them to the canteen for lunch. I'm grateful when they try to speak English with me because my brain is feeling thoroughly overwhelmed. They all look like they're wearing a uniform of their own choosing: blue jeans that tuck into boots, plain tops and jackets.

Like the *directrice* said, I have to show my ID card and

also scan my hand (what?!) in a machine, which shoots out a tray, and then I can choose my lunch. I follow the girls to a salad bar and a hot lunch station (potato, chicken, carrots and brussels sprouts).

'Does anyone bring their lunch from home?' I ask.

'In France it's forbidden to bring your own lunch,' says the girl with braids, whose name I have already forgotten.

'It's better like this,' says one of the others, whose gold hoop earrings are so impressively big they almost touch her shoulders. 'We all eat the same thing. It is more fair.'

This makes sense, even though it blows my mind. I think about my old life, and its regular lunch of a cheese sandwich, apple and maybe a little packet of Barbecue Shapes. In my new life, I eat my way through a three-course meal, including dessert. Today it is yoghurt.

'Sometimes we will have fruit or *mousse au chocolat*,' says the braids girl. (How do I ask her name again without being rude?)

We're all in the same class all the time, basically, and we all study the same core subjects: Maths, French, English, Histoire-Géo (history-geography), Science, and everyone has to study another language as well. 'It is good,' says one of the other girls, 'because we can help you find your way.'

'The *directrice* has put me in German class,' I tell them. 'I am scared of the first class! I know nothing!'

The girls laugh, so I laugh along.

After lunch we go outside and stand around in the concrete courtyard. A bunch of kids kick a soccer ball around, and the game and the shouting and the cold air are alienating. I feel alien.

The girls lead me over to a small group that I recognise from class. '*Bonjour,*' I say, being quite brave.

'Amandine, Victor, Hassan ...'

I try to keep track as I am introduced to a semi-circle of faces.

'*T'es la petite Australienne?*'

'*Euh. Oui?*'

They try to speak English to me. I can't decide if I like it or feel frustrated by it.

They look me up and down and I start to feel kind of uncomfortable.

'Doctor Martens,' says one of the guys, who has a shaved head, looking at my feet. 'You are punk? Punk music?'

'Not really,' I reply, but the next person along is already talking.

'What kind of music do you like? Do you like French music? Tell us one French singer what you know!'

'You must be rich to do exchange. Are they all rich, the Australians?'

I don't know how to respond. I have also never patted a kangaroo, and I don't know how to surf. I hope they'll find something interesting about me at some point. I've never been great at making friends.

'Did you have a nice day?' asks the girl with the braids, as students surge up the concrete steps and through the front door onto the street. I am so grateful for her sticking by me all day. It is 5 pm and I am exhausted.

'Yes, thank you,' I reply.

'And you like Paris, *hein*?'

I pull my beanie onto my head. 'It's a bit cold,' I say. My brain feels like it is about to explode. It is already night-time, the sky low and the streetlights on. Will I be able to find my way back to the house? No time for navigation worries. I have to make like an explorer. Challenge accepted.

The girl smiles and zips up her puffer jacket. '*Salut! À demain, Sofie.*' Bye! See you tomorrow, Sofie.

'*À demain!*' I call back. A friend! But what is her name again?

'Leia!' a guy calls. My new friend turns towards him. '*On va faire un MacDo! Tu viens?*'

(I realise later that her name isn't Leia, like the space princess. It is *Léa*.)

That night, after my first day at my new French school, I lie awake in my borrowed bed, and sleep isn't going to happen. I draw my day like a map – the grim school building, the classes, the classmates. After I've recorded my day my mind turns to home, and I draw the flight path again, going Paris to Melbourne this time. I label the distances. I draw in the time zones. One hundred and forty days until I go home.

I decide to call these drawings my Lonely Homesick Maps. I think about posting them to my feed, but then I decide not to share them online in case I worry my parents and Hana. She's done so much to get me here. They all have. *I've* done so much to get me here.

I draw my house, back home. Next to it, I draw the apartment here. *I should send this to Mum and Dad*, I think, temporarily forgetting I can take a photo.

I draw a rope ladder from my Paris window.

I draw a person, waiting at the bottom of the rope ladder.

A handsome someone. With dark curly hair.

A someone I had spied today in the hallway of my new school.

8

I am definitely more occupied with nerves about drawing in front of people than I am about fitting in during my first drawing class with the *Arts Plastiques* group. We meet in the school's *atelier de peinture* – the art studio.

Where the rest of the school kind of lacks personality (although even now, on day two, I am getting glimpses of life here and there), the atelier seems to welcome me with warm and open arms. I mean, it smells the same as the art classroom back home – of paint and turpentine – but here there truly is an aroma of imagination and possibility.

Back home, the art classroom was fine and had everything I needed, but it was dark and poky. The atelier is a large open space with heavy-looking wooden tables and a row of easels. There's shambolic shelving and racks for drying and a big window for light. I am already in love with it.

I meet Pauline and Paul and Victor and Fatima. I recognise some of them from my other classes.

I've worn my black dress with a belt for today's class.

I drew winged eyeliner on. But I put my clothes, my hair, my face out of my mind. I am here for the ART.

Or I think I am, before a latecomer lopes in. Dark curly hair. Black button-down shirt with a pair of black jeans. My heart skips a beat and I remember yesterday – the most beautiful boy I've seen outside of the movies, holding a hardback book in his hand and speaking to a friend in the hallway. When I walked past, he glanced over and smiled at me. His smile caused molten gold to run through my blood.

Now, as he takes his seat, I wrench my attention back to class and will my heart to beat at a regular pace and the heat in my veins to cool.

'Good morning, everyone!' Véronique, art teacher and friend of Léon, is almost exactly what I had wished for in an art teacher in France – stately, with long hair twirled up into a bun, wearing a simple-but-surely-expensive black shift dress (see! My outfit is right!) and some small silver earrings.

I discover pretty quickly that I have a real gift for interpreting body language and gestures if I don't understand the words being said. Maybe it's all that time I've spent, as Crow says, being 'a weird little watching creeper'. I am a watcher and Crow is a thinker. I guess that's why we've stayed friends all this time – we don't mind the other just disappearing into reverie, dreamworld or spiral. I have always liked to observe what's going on before I act, or at least I find it useful. Also, the French are terrific at gestures and facial expressions. The pursed lips, a little puff of air released between them, more a *ppt* than a *pfft*.

We sketch in this first class – still life mostly. 'This is a simple task,' says Véronique, conducting a piece of charcoal through the air as she speaks, 'but one to take seriously.'

I breathe in the smell of charcoal. I smooth my paper beneath my hand. I am happy with my apple, but I'm having trouble with my pear. I'm finding it hard to make it look realistic and not lopsided. The fat end is easy because that's quite apple-ish, but as I move towards the end with the stalk on it, it's harder to capture. It's so frustrating – my skills have always been in the detail.

'This is not bad,' says a voice over my shoulder.

I scrunch my face up at Véronique. 'I must practise.'

'All the world must practise,' she says. (I realise later that she meant 'everyone', not 'all the world'. *Tout le monde*. That's an expression *I know*! Argh, come on, brain.)

The class turns to look.

'Please forgive my faults,' I say. They laugh, just a little bit. What mistake have I made now? 'I am Australian,' I say. 'It's only my second day at school in France.'

We look at each other's work. 'But we do not compare ourselves; we just compare what we have done to what we will do,' Véronique reminds us sternly. I want to say, 'Please forgive my faults' again, but I just do a little half-smile (a *Mona Lisa* smile!) and admire my classmates' work.

Some of them are at a similar level to mine. Pear-ish, apple-ish. Some have better shading; others have better shape. Some are much better than mine.

I watch the curly-haired boy brush charcoal off his hands and I ogle his still life, which is absolutely amazing. Perfect. His apple is an apple – I feel like I could reach out and pluck it from the page. It wouldn't even taste of charcoal; it would be sweet and tangy. He's even managed to make his pear a pear!

While we are packing up, I can't help but sneak looks at him. I feel self-conscious and I wonder how *I* am coming across to them all, but especially to *him*. I can't stop thinking about how he is A. Very. Good. Looking. Person.

And I watch him brush charcoal off his hands again, and I ogle, and I *feel something*.

'I like your apple, *p'tit kangourou*,' he says, maybe noticing me staring (how embarrassing!). 'Your pear could use some work, but it's not bad.'

Yes. I am definitely feeling *things*.

'Thank you,' I say. 'Your pear is perfect.'

We smile at each other. He thinks my apple is good! So much smiling.

'Me, I'm Olivier,' he says. *Olivier.*

For a near-constant daydreamer, I'm astonished to realise I have never felt less in my body than I do right now. 'I'm Sofie,' I manage to say.

Véronique has disappeared from the atelier, and the other students are milling about, some leaving, some putting their drawings in large folios so they can carry them home.

I try to bring myself back to the ground, and I tap softly (respectfully) on Olivier's folio, an expensive-looking brown leather, which he is closing up with a zipper that goes around and around. 'This is really nice,' I say. The leather is so smooth under my finger that I know it is way out of my price range.

'It was a gift from my grandmother,' he replies.

'Olivier, I'm going,' says a girl with long black hair.

She is wearing a woollen dress, and I think her name is Amandine. She is friends with Léa.

'*À tout de suite*,' he replies. Be right there.

'Bye, Sofie,' she says in English. Her tone is friendly but her face is serious.

'What do you think of our atelier?' Olivier asks, gesturing about with his hands. I notice his long fingers and neat, perfect fingernails. We are the last two people left in the classroom.

I look around again in wonder. 'It's incredible,' I say. 'I am going to make great art in here.'

He rests one of those very same hands, with its pianist fingers, on my arm for just a moment, and laughs. 'I like this confidence.'

I'm momentarily embarrassed to come across as arrogant, but just smile like I meant to say it.

'What is your preferred material?' he asks me. I must look confused (I am) because he adds, 'What kind of art – sorry, great art – do you like to make?'

'I like to draw. My pear was a little sad today, but I do mostly like to make realistic pencil drawings. I love the little details.' I really *do* feel that I can create great art in this space.

'For me,' he says, 'I love painting.' He pushes off the bench and heads to the other side of the room, where there are huge wooden shelves for storing canvases.

'Oh, so do I,' I say, following. In the back of my mind I'm also buzzing – I am *speaking French* with *a French person* and we're talking about *things that matter to us*. This is what I came here for!

'I am going to make my piece for the exhibition in oils,' Olivier says, pulling down a canvas and running his hand across it before turning it around for me to see.

It's a half-finished painting, but astonishing even so. It's the shadowy corner of a room, material draping down one side – perhaps a curtain – and the arms and torso of a person – a woman – sitting in an armchair, wearing a thin dress that dips into all her curves. The way the skin is painted is so realistic I can practically see the hair on her arms. The top half of the painting is still a sketch, but you can see her hand holding something up (a mirror?). He's planning her face in profile, and she's beautiful. I wonder if she's a real person.

'This is your painting?' I ask, pointing and hoping it doesn't sound rude.

Olivier smiles (his smile is dazzling). 'Yes. I'm trying to capture the Romantic style, but make it modern. You see?' He points to the rough box the woman is holding. 'Here I will have her holding her phone.'

'Oh, this is clever,' I say. I feel, suddenly, like I am wasting my time with my current medium of pen and pencil and the occasional acrylic paint. Not to mention my unclever re-creations of tiny beautifuls – I've not thought to subvert a classic style and make it modern.

'And the exhibition, what's that?' I ask.

'In May we will be showing our work in an exhibition at the École des Beaux-Arts. It's a type of audition. Professors and artists from the university will be able to see our work.'

My head spins. For all my dreaming and planning

over the past twelve months, there is still so little I have anticipated. I hope I'll be allowed to take part in the exhibition. I hope I'll get to know Olivier better.

Olivier slides his canvas back onto the shelf, smiles at me and says, 'Okay, well, until next time.'

'Until next time,' I say, sorry to see him go. But I stand here, in the now-empty atelier, and the next five months roll out ahead of me paved with possibility.

9

The first week in Paris goes by both in a flash and at a crawl.

Claudette seems so much more artistic than Léon, when he's supposed to be the artist. I'm still not entirely sure what her job is – something in a gallery – but she gets up quite early and wears sharp outfits with beautiful, bright scarves or neat blazers (or both, sometimes). She plays music in whichever room she's in, sometimes in multiple rooms. For a tiny flat they have a lot of radios and bluetooth speakers.

My mum sings along to the radio, usually pretty badly. Claudette isn't like that, but you can tell she's really listening to the music.

I have never eaten so much food in my life. Every morning I have a breakfast *tartine* – bread with butter and jam. Claudette makes me a hot chocolate while she makes coffee for the rest of the family. Then there are the school lunches – always a hot meal, always a dessert.

We have dinner as a family each night. I find myself eating things I don't like very much, but unable to say anything because it's too impolite. One night we eat a quiche and the egg is wibbling and the ham is extra hammy and have you ever had that feeling of being drawn inside yourself, where it's a battle between you and the food? You go a bit deaf until you manage to get it down.

Delphine is in and out of the apartment like a spy. I hardly see her. When I do, she's friendly, though private. Her bedroom door is nearly always closed. I did get a peek in one morning as we crossed paths to the bathroom, and I greedily took in the sight: a keyboard piano with headphones resting on top, two pairs of running shoes lined up by the wardrobe, and a big indoor plant soaking up the winter sun.

True to their word, Claudette and Léon speak only French with me. I'm happy with how much I understand, and I'm finding it easier to express myself, but it's exhausting. Sometimes when I go to bed, I want to cry with how tired I am and how my head constantly aches.

Crow messages on Saturday morning: *Go do something beautiful.* It is so unlike her. Usually she's stuck in the gloomy and the negative. But she is right.

So, because of my quest for beauty, and because I have twenty euros burning a hole in my pocket, I stop at a bakery and buy a *pain au chocolat* and I head out into the city. I eat it as I walk (which later I find out is a bit of a faux-pas, a French no-no) and the buttery, flaky pastry and the bitter sweetness of the chocolate melt together in my mouth.

I am keeping a list of my expenses so far (most outgoings fall under 'croissant' or '*pain au chocolat*'). I am under my budget thanks to all the home-cooked meals and me walking places instead of taking the metro. School is a twenty-minute walk, and apart from that first day I haven't really gone further afield.

As well as redefining my Parisian style, I have been planning my route around the galleries and museums for at least a year. Maybe longer. The Louvre, the Musée d'Orsay, the Centre Pompidou. Monet's garden out in Giverny. I am looking forward to being able to pronounce *Giverny.*

I want to see that famous half-smiling *Mona Lisa.*

If you are an adult, it's a bit expensive to get into the Louvre, but my greatest joy is finding out that entry for people under the age of eighteen is completely free!

I thank my lingering jet lag stars for waking me up early. I listen to music as I walk to the train; I've been bingeing on Spotify French playlists ever since I found out I was going on exchange. Playlists that seem to either be whispery sexy women speak-singing over a jazzy piano track, or fastfastfast rapping.

Crow likes the rapping, but she absolutely hates the whispers and says they give her the creeps. 'The French are obsessed with having people think they're sexy,' she had said, and pretended to vom. 'When in reality they eat really weird things – like, have you ever looked at a snail? – that are not sexy at all.'

So I listen to the rap. I like the way it makes me saunter, makes me feel brave, makes my feet feel confident in where they're going.

~

Where I'm going I have to take the brown 11 metro towards Châtelet. While I'm waiting for the train, Delphine texts me: *Are you at the museum yet?* (I had left a note on the kitchen table. I hadn't tried to imitate the loopy French handwriting, but I did leave a doodle of me looking at the *Mona Lisa*.) I hadn't expected to hear from her, but it makes me feel warm and cared-for.

The train arrives and once I've found a seat, I text back: *Not yet. Just getting on the metro.*

Be careful, sends Delphine. *When you get off the train, it's easy to go the wrong way down at Châtelet–Les Halles. Those metro tunnels are labyrinthine hallways – you walk for 10 full minutes and end up in completely the wrong place.*

I had already decided to be careful. The tile-and-concrete design of the metro stations we pass brings to mind toilet blocks, bunkers or psychiatric hospitals. I slip my phone back into my bag – still careful with my things on the metro – and in my mind I'm sketching a new connection from me to my host sister. A line growing and stretching out like a little vine. I hope it gets stronger.

Once at the Louvre and through the security checks – of course, in spite of myself – I beeline for the *Mona Lisa* and of course, in the cliché of clichés, she's already surrounded by adoring crowds.

It still gives me a thrill to glimpse her.

We learned last year in class that da Vinci made up a special technique called *sfumato* to create the light and the depths in this painting. By blending the paint together, he created an effect that's somehow *more real than real.*

The lines between colours and brushstrokes disappear like smoke. *Fumo* is Italian for smoke. (In French, smoke is *la fumée*.)

I didn't expect so many of the crowding masses to be as interested in *sfumato* and painterly magic, and so I wander off to look at whatever catches my eye. I almost gasp at the physical size of some of the paintings, and I wonder if they were ever intended to be hung inside people's houses. There are some taller than our ceilings at home and many more that wouldn't fit through the doorways … unless you unframed them and rolled them up. I wonder if that's how they had transported them for safekeeping during the Nazi occupation of Paris?

Imagine having all these paintings in your home. That's my dream for the future. Tall walls and art everywhere.

Each piece of art in the Louvre sends my heart and soul flying. *Liberty Leading the People. The Raft of the Medusa. The Lacemaker*, hard at her work. They're famous, iconic, historical. And here I am, with so much beauty around me I can't believe it.

And the statues! I already knew about *Psyche Revived by Cupid's Kiss* and the *Venus de Milo*. And they're stunning, although their smooth white surfaces give off a cold feeling that I hadn't expected. I love seeing them (tick – there's a dream come true; tick – there's another), but they don't move me like I thought they would.

However, when I see the *Winged Victory of Samothrace* I just stand there, beguiled, taken out of myself for a good minute. I see the top of her first, as I come up the stairs, just the tips of her wings. Then, the rest.

She's a headless woman – well, she would have had a head originally, but she's lost it somewhere along the way – with magnificent wings spread out behind her, her chest high and proud. She's made of stone, but she's also wrapped in drapes of cloth. How is this stonework so strong and intricate, and so full of movement?

She is extraordinary and I want, all of a sudden, to take up stonework and carving.

Am I allowed to touch? (Probably not.) I compromise by sitting and sketching her, attempting to capture her strength and her steadfastness. I sketch from each angle. I take a photo. I resketch.

I brush a lot of eraser crumbies onto the floor of the Louvre this first visit. I'm clearly leaving an impression on Paris already.

10

Sofie

Crow, it was amazing to see the
Louvre. But I'm so tired. Maybe
I want to come home?

Crow

Don't come home. You've only seen
one gallery. Aren't there like fifty?

Ha. Probably. But I can't speak
French, I'm practically in the suburbs,
I don't know how to talk to my host
family, their daughter's hardly ever here,
everyone at school thinks I'm boring.

Yes, but you're in Paris. What's
it like? It must be beautiful.

Well, this neighbourhood is pretty grey
and concrete. It's kind of desolate.

Never thought you'd call Paris desolate.

Shut up.

– Overnight chats with Crow

Sunday rolls around, and I struggle to wake up. The morning light coming in my window is dim and gloomy. Even though things are going well, objectively, I suddenly find myself weary and a little bit sad. It's extremely uncomfortable, especially considering how hard I worked to get here.

The apartment is in a grey building in a street of grey buildings. I've seen films about East Berlin, and these are the kind of buildings you'd have seen there. Okay, so some of the buildings have small iron Juliet balconies and window boxes that promise flowers in the spring, but the few trees I can see are bare.

I should have expected this, since it is January and January here means mid-winter.

A little bit of homesickness stabs me and the aftershocks echo with a feeling of creeping disappointment. Maybe this isn't going to be everything I had been dreaming of?

I message home, but I don't let them know my wobbles. I reassure them I am alive, eating, safe and warm.

I feel both worried I am wasting my time and impatient for the exchange to be over. And I'm confused at how I can even feel these two competing feelings at the same time. I remind myself this is only my first week. Well, I guess technically now it's my second. Still. I have all the time in the world. And there is still so long to go.

I don't think I've ever felt alone or abandoned. Mum says

on my first day of school, I held her hand and accepted her hug and just as easily accepted her leaving – off I went to the classroom with Mr Rose and all the other little preppies.

But I feel tired in France. I feel lonely here, too. Lonely! I've never felt this before. It's not like I surround myself with lots of people, generally – but I miss my house, my parents, Hana, Crow. I miss feeling like part of the furniture. I want someone to chat with, to hang out with, to laugh with. I like that Delphine texted me yesterday, and I hope she'll be around a bit more.

Preparing for this trip had involved my whole family, though I was responsible for paying for it – Mum and Dad made that clear right from the start.

I'd made an extra effort to focus in French class, and I labelled things in the house, so we all learned that *le frigo* is the fridge, *un couteau* is a knife and *la fenêtre* is the window. Dad loved his three trips a week to *la piscine*. He also loved laughing a lot when he said *piscine* ('piss-in').

I wish there was someone here I could laugh about the piss-in with.

'What are you going to do today?' Léon asks over a hot chocolate at breakfast.

Part of me wants to say, 'Nothing,' and just lie in bed doodling all day, but it feels like a really lazy option. By the time I'd gotten up, Delphine was already gone, to running club, according to Claudette.

I had kind of hoped Delphine might want to show me around.

'I think I'll go for a walk to explore the *quartier*,' I say.

The streets crisscross and take off at angles that make me think I'm heading in completely the wrong direction, but somehow, I turn a corner and things make sense again. Anyway, I don't really mind getting lost.

As I walk, I video chat with home.

'*Bonjour*, my daughter!' Dad's voice booms through my headphones as his face appears on the screen.

'Hi! My brain hurts! I'm so tired!' I flop onto a park bench. It makes me feel so weirdly happy to see his face beaming at me, too close to the camera eye on the phone.

'Why does your brain hurt?' Dad asks, clearly concerned (he has excessively expressive eyebrows).

'From speaking all this French, of course!' I throw my free arm emphatically, forgetting I am in public. I should lower my voice, probably.

'That's great, Sof!' says Mum, as a disembodied voice coming from somewhere behind him. 'Your French must be getting so good.'

'Not yet,' I say. 'It's hard. But what's happening at home?'

'Oh, nothing's changed.'

'It's been a week!'

'I know. It's only been a week. You've ignored us in a huff longer than this.'

Rude! But true. It's just the distance is hard. I feel funny talking about it. 'Have you seen Hana?' I say instead. 'Has she come over?'

'That girl!' Mum shakes her head. 'Still in that job.'

'What's the daughter like?' asks Dad, changing the subject.

I pull my knees up and balance my phone on one of them.

'Delphine? I'm not really sure. I've hardly seen her. She's always on her phone or she's off running. She's in a running club. I don't think she wants to hang around with me.'

I talk to my parents for long enough to remember that they ask a million ridiculous questions and they talk over the top of each other all the time. It's really freakin' annoying, so I tell them I have to go. I love them, I do, but it is getting rapidly easier being away from them!

Belleville is a very hilly part of the city, unlike the *centre ville* of Paris you see in the pictures, so as well as crisscrossing I am all up and down.

Crow is back online.

Isn't it all je ne sais quoi and frou frou with a croissant on top? she messages.

No! I text back. *I actually think you'd like this area more than I do. It's grungy and dirty and covered in graffiti.*

And what about the people at school? Anyone not awful and pompous?

They seem nice. The teachers make them look after me and they speak better English than I do.

Stop worrying, she texts back. *You're going to be fine.*

Who is this person? Back at home, sometimes Crow wouldn't be around at lunchtime because she'd go to the library or somewhere else where there weren't many people, and she'd despair on her own. She'd read the news and follow Reddit threads all the way to their murky bottoms; she'd sympathise with conspiracy theorists, and she'd fret.

Found the love of your life yet?

Maybe.

TELL!

There's nothing to tell. He's in my art class and I told him I thought his pear was very pear-like.

I can't believe you didn't say it was pear-fect, writes Crow.

WE WERE SPEAKING IN FRENCH!

I walk without thinking and before I know it, I've walked halfway across the city.

I stand on the Pont des Arts, where students wrapped in coats linger like lovers (they surely are lovers, some of them). They are leaning on the railings, embracing on the bench seats dotted along this bridge, and I feel super alone. But we are all also watching the *bateaux mouches*, the boats that carry tourists along the Seine, and we are all surrounded by the wintry afternoon light. I'm watching the *bateaux* and the light, but I am also mostly people-watching, of course.

My fingers, gloved in wool, curl around the railing of the bridge. The other hand is entwined nervously in the strap of my handbag, a small corner of my thoughts on pickpockets still.

Though it's only four o'clock in the afternoon the sky is darkening, the sun descending towards the horizon. In the distance there is a cluster of skyscrapers. They're so not in keeping with the rest of the city's aesthetic, and I wonder how the French can bear their ugliness.

I've read about this bridge. Lovers used to put padlocks on it as symbols of their love, especially near Valentine's Day – *le jour de la Saint Valentin*.

Perhaps I'll have met someone by Valentine's Day? Perhaps I will have found someone amazing.

You can't put locks on the bridge anymore – there are big perspex sheets all along the sides.

The weight of people's love was threatening to topple the bridge into the Seine.

11

Sofie

Did you know that snowflakes are fluffy?

Crow

Are you really talking to me about snowflakes?

What else do you want to know?

Can you take some more photos of the graffiti for me? Maybe I'll take up tagging.

Are you looking at my Insta???

… so what if I am?

– Overnight chats with Crow

I have now been in France for two weeks. Fourteen days. I have Instagrammed the following things:

1. Selfie, with view out of my new bedroom window.

2. Les Champs-Élysées (and Insta stories of our day).
3. Jaunty Eiffel Tower shot.
4. Selfie, post first-day-of-school, me posing cross-eyed.
5. Croissant, close up, laid on a thin tissue paper – direct from the *boulangerie* (purchased on the walk to school).
6. Hot chocolate on a green table at a café near school.
7. The Louvre! The *Mona Lisa*!
8. More photos from the Louvre.
9. Selfie, with snowflakes falling.
10. Time-lapse video as I walk from the Moulin Rouge to the Sacré Cœur.
11. My feet in a puddle of dirty, melted snow on the streets.
12. Street cleaner, in his green outfit and with his funny green sweeper.
13. Scungy graffiti.
14. Dog poop on the footpath.

You could be fooled into thinking everything was croissants and *bonheur* (well, apart from the poop), but it felt good to post beautiful, funny things on my feed. Things that people would expect. Maybe I can also fool myself into believing I'm not flailing here.

I'm struggling in my *Arts Plastiques* class. First of all, having school on a Saturday morning seems very rude. 'This is not bad work, Sofie,' Véronique says, tracing the lines on my paper with a manicured fingernail. 'But you can do better, I think. Stop thinking so much.'

I'm not sure how to stop thinking. I just look down at my work. Our task is to draw a human face. We have a mix of magazines, photographs, facsimiles of paintings and drawings and cartoons to take inspiration from.

'You seem to worry about making mistakes. Just let the pencil sketch freely.' Véronique gives a sweep of her arm, and repeats the action, saying, 'Free. Loose. Let yourself fail.'

I'm struggling to make friends. After school I walk out of the gates and, in the café across the road, I spy Olivier. I look again and realise I'm spying Olivier and all of the other people from our *Arts Plastiques* class. Why wasn't I invited too? Then at the same time, Léa turns to me and says, 'I'm sorry, I am late to meet my brother.' And she runs off.

I stand there feeling rejected and dejected and decidedly square-peggish. I could go over and sit with my class, but I just can't push my feet that way.

Go and do something beautiful, Crow had said. I mentally check through my Paris must-dos. We are studying *la Révolution francaise* at school (well, the rest of my class is, and I try to follow as best I can), so the next port of call in my on-foot discoveries of Paris has to be the Bastille.

Upon arriving, I can't deny I am disappointed to find it merely a large roundabout with a tall column stretching skyward. *This* is all that's left to signify the great prison and commemorate the day that the commoners (the Third Estate) committed an act (storming the prison) that would snowball into revolution and overthrow the monarchy?

I sit on the concrete ledge of the Bassin de l'Arsenal, eat the croissant I bought on the way and stare at the cars tootling around.

There's an iconic painting of the storming of the Bastille – the artist Jean-Pierre Houël depicted it in watercolours of gloomy grey and blues. It's epic. But also, I know from Wikipedia there were only seven prisoners in the Bastille prison when it was stormed by the partisans.

My croissant finished, I jump down from the ledge and, at random, pick a road running off from the Place de la Bastille and start wandering. On a lightbox bus stop advertisement there's some scrawled graffiti in sharp black lettering: *Macron démission! Stop aux pillages du peuple.* Resign Macron! Stop stealing from the people.

In my mind I see President Emmanuel Macron dressed as King Louis XVI. He was the Louis with Marie Antoinette for a wife, and the one the revolution was brought against, the same revolution that saw this mighty monarchy brought to its knees (brought to its knees on the guillotine!).

Crow always talks about the widening gap between the rich and the poor, but thinking about the French Revolution in the context of today's issues makes it seem more real. Even here, in this place where history seems to have been replaced by a column. In the whole time we've studied the revolution, I've never thought about it this way. It's easy to be distracted by the wigs and the dresses and the two hundred and thirty years.

The graffiti (I think left by the *gilets jaunes*) makes me think of Crow and, suddenly, I miss her terribly.

I send her a message: *What are you doing today? I am*

forcing myself to do some sightseeing and I just want to speak some English!

We've been texting each other every day, but I'm a little surprised when a reply message bips through almost right away.

You poor thing stuck in Paris. How awful.

Isn't it one in the morning there? I write.

I can't sleep. Too hot.

Meanwhile I'm wearing tights under my jeans again, and my cheeks are numb.

It's freezing here. I feel miserable.

I see a sign that says: '*Promenade Plantée/Coulée verte René-Dumont*'. I have heard about this. I walk up the steps and onto a boardwalk. It's an old elevated train line that's been converted into a long stretch of garden and pathway. There aren't many people out on the *coulée.* Not many plants either.

And then my phone rings and it's Crow calling. What the heck? I answer, almost nervously. 'What's going on? Are you okay?'

'Yeah,' she says, like I'm an idiot. I've missed her croaky voice. 'But what about you?'

My heart swamps with self-pity. 'Crow, it's really hard. I'm exhausted. My host family is nice, but they're not my family. And … Oh, I dunno.'

I am glad we are speaking on the phone. It feels easier to speak honestly and directly from my heart to hers.

'I get it.' We are silent together for a moment. She doesn't say, *But you wanted to go.* She doesn't say anything. I look out from the promenade, through the bare spindly arms of a tree to an intersection and some cars with their headlights on in the dimming afternoon light.

'How's the gorgeous art boy?'

I can't be too miserable at the way my body reacts to the thought of Olivier.

'He's so gorgeous, Crow. Today we talked about how Vermeer painted in a camera obscura to get his paintings to have that photorealistic effect.'

'That means nothing to me.' Crow's bluntness hasn't bothered me since I was six.

'I know. But Crow, when I leaned in a spot of oil paint, he went and got a cloth to help me clean it off.'

'Dreamboat,' she says, dryly but with kindness.

'But I just feel like ... everyone in my art class is so incredibly talented, and I'm worried I won't be able to, like, match them or live up to expectations. I'm scared I'm no good. And' – because now I'm on a roll – 'why am I even here if I'm no good?'

I miss home, suddenly, intensely. I wonder what Crow is looking at. 'Where are you? What's it like there?'

'It's one in the morning. I'm in my bedroom. Where do you think I am? It's so hot here.' She is quiet for a minute and I try to think of something to say, but then she goes on. 'What's it like where you are?'

'I've just found the *Promenade Plantée*, even though I wasn't even looking for it. To be honest, for a "green path" it's not very green. Everything looks dead,' I say with a bitter kind of ironic laugh because I am truly a little disappointed.

'So what are you going to do now?' she asks.

'I'm just going to walk along this alleged green path – *Coulée verte* – until I get tired.'

'Where does it come out?'

'I have no idea.' I genuinely don't. I figure finding out is part of today's adventure.

'Well, don't get lost,' she says.

I'm glad she can't see my face because I am grinning and I wouldn't want her to think I was laughing at her. 'If I don't know where I'm going or if I'm going nowhere in particular, how can I be lost?'

'I'm joking,' she adds. 'I'm looking at a map online and I know exactly where you are.'

'Don't tell me.'

'I won't.'

'I saw some good graffiti. I'll send it to you.' I've been taking photos of all the political scrawls on walls and bus stops. It's been good for learning new vocab as I translate them into English. 'The yellow vests have been out most weekends.'

'Sounds like my kind of place.'

'Thank you for calling me,' I say.

'Bye, Sof.'

'Bye, Crow.'

I am doing okay, I think to myself. The plants along this path may look dead, but I've read *The Secret Garden* enough times to know they're just waiting for the spring.

The late-afternoon sunshine lights up the buildings, with their cream and white sides and their tiny wrought-iron balconies and their dainty tiled roofs, and I'm mostly walking in shadow, the cold almost freezing my nose off.

But those buildings and that light! What dreams they must contain.

Shadow and light. The bad illuminated by the good. No, that's not quite right – the good warming and illuminating things. It makes my heart happy. The fear I'm not where I'm supposed to be dissipates.

There are a million more galleries to look at, streets to walk down, people to meet, secrets to find, and maybe even the possibility of boys (one boy in particular) to kiss. I feel my confidence and the part of me that believes in dreams start to bolster.

And then it starts snowing. Actual snow falls, and flakes land on my hands and my coat. I will never get enough of this.

I take the time to film snowflakes falling, on bare branches, on leaves, on my sleeves. This might cool Crow down. Then I post it to Instagram too because you never know who might need to see snow falling at any given time.

12

'What are you doing tomorrow?' Delphine asks when I get back to the apartment from my long saunter down the Coulée verte. Delphine is lying on the sofa, her feet up on the armrest. She's working on her laptop, typing while she talks. She always speaks English with me and I'm not sure if I'm supposed to respond in English or French.

English obviously wins out. 'I'm not sure. It's really cold.' I perch on the edge of one of the couches, unsure if I should settle in or if I'm interrupting her.

'Maybe you could go to the Musée d'Orsay? It's free entry.'

I nod, not sure whether I will have the energy to leave the house again tomorrow if I don't have to. I rub my hands together, not sure if my fingers will ever heat up again. I can't believe I'm being blasé about the Musée d'Orsay! But then again, I've never had the chance to say, 'Oh well, I'll go another day.'

'You really should go to the museum. I think you'll love it. I could come with you,' she says.

I sit back against the cushions and tuck my feet up

underneath me, feeling warmer already. 'That sounds really good.'

So Delphine and I take the metro together, and it's the first time I've caught the metro with someone else since that first day when Claudette pushed me from the train like she believed in my independence.

Delphine doesn't talk much while we're on the metro. But it's not an awkward silence at all; when our arms bump as the train rattles through the dark, Delphine's amused smile is friendly, and I feel like I've made another big step in befriending Paris, another step towards making it my home. If I don't open my mouth, maybe the other passengers will just assume I have always lived here. Today I pass as a local – a local with a friend! – and it is so much more exciting than I could have hoped.

The Musée d'Orsay is right near the river Seine, on the left bank. We must have walked past it on our orientation, but I think I had been too distracted by the river and the jet-lagged-newness. Toby surely would have pointed it out.

It's on my list of essential places to visit: an old train station transformed into an art gallery of (mostly) French Impressionist and Post-Impressionist art. Crow would say (in a monotone): *Well, I'm very impressed-ionist right now.*

We come back up to street level, and the buildings around here are postcard-perfect, I swear. We're not in Belleville anymore.

We line up to enter the museum and, while we wait, Delphine asks, 'So you never finished telling me why you decided to do this exchange?'

Here's how it happened.

Hana had come over for dinner to do her washing (like I said, it is a common occurrence). I was rinsing my paintbrushes in the kitchen sink.

'So,' said Hana, 'I was reading about this foreign exchange program for Australian high school students, and I thought Sof might be interested in doing a five-month exchange in France.'

France. In a split second I was there! The Eiffel Tower! The *Mona Lisa*! Dark jazz clubs. Baguettes. Croissants. Striped t-shirts.

Okay, so all the images flicking through my head were from movies and songs and *ideas* of France. Because how could France be possible? It was so far out of reality's reach I actually couldn't properly *imagine* it.

Dad didn't even put his book down. 'Sounds great, Han.'

I'd heard about people's hearts leaping in their chest and always thought it was metaphorical, but had I been in an MRI machine the doctor would have seen my genuine anatomical heart take a quick jump towards my chin.

'Are you okay with not eating for a year or so, Annie?' he asked, peering over the top of the pages.

'We could stop paying our bills too, Pete,' Mum replied, her voice sharp with sarcasm. 'Why not? France is worth it.'

'Well, fortunately, I'm bringing it up because I'm offering to help pay for her to go,' said Hana.

There was silence around the lounge room. Mum and Dad looked at Hana. Hana looked at me. I looked from each one to the other.

I didn't even care they were talking about me in front of

me. For once, I didn't feel the need to shout, 'Hey! I'm here, you know!' I think I realised at that point that this could actually truly happen if the next few minutes went well.

'That's very generous, darling,' said Mum in a voice completely different to before. 'But wouldn't you prefer to spend your money moving somewhere a bit nicer? A bit safer?'

'Or maybe change jobs? You could earn less but do something you like.' Dad took every chance he got to jab Hana about her job.

'I'm fine where I am for now, work-wise. And you know I love my place.'

Hana explained the program. 'And the exchange kids are from all around the world – not just Aussie kids. It's kind of the luck of the draw where in the country you get placed, but even if you're in a little hick town there's still opportunities to travel. And apparently your language skills will take right off.'

'And how do you know so much about it?' Dad asked.

'There's a family scholarship that's allied with my company,' she said, dismissively, with a classic Hana flap of the hand. 'Don't you remember how much I wanted to go on exchange? I'd like to give Sofie that chance. If she wants to, of course.'

I remember when she wanted to go. I was little, and the idea of her going away for months and months was terrifying, but also a little bit thrilling. I'd never known you could leave your family and have adventures by yourself.

Mum smooshed Hana into a hug. 'I'm sorry you couldn't go.'

Hana wriggled free. 'Get off. It's fine.' Turning to me, she asked, 'So what do you think?'

I was thinking so many things. 'Don't you want to use your money to travel yourself?'

Hana shrugged. 'I'll get around to it. Don't think about the money. With the scholarship it's really not going to be that bad. I want to help you. And you've got a year or whatever to save up. Sell more cards or get a job.'

I could do those things, I thought.

Croissants.

The Eiffel Tower.

The Louvre!

THE MUSÉE D'ORSAY.

I couldn't get 'yes' out fast enough.

And now here I am. At the Musée d'Orsay.

I tell Delphine this story and she is interested in my sister. She asks questions about Hana in that very polite, non-invasive French way. 'What does your sister study? Oh, she has finished university? She's fortunate to have found such a good job. Do you get along well together, in spite of the age difference?'

The French are very private people. We've learned this in class (I think it was even part of last year's assignment on French society). They have over 400 official cheeses, and they don't like to overstep boundaries. They kiss near-strangers hello, but rarely invite people into their homes unless they're very good friends.

~

We have to wait in the Musée d'Orsay line for about twenty minutes, but between Delphine's questions and my stories it doesn't feel too long. Then we are in. I gaze around, and you'd think I'd be used to this by now: seeing something with my very own eyes that up until now I've seen only in photos, my textbooks and on the internet. But no.

'Is there something that you particularly want to see?' asks Delphine.

But I am seeing everything already. This magnificent building! The white stone, the arched glass roof curving overhead. The high, high ceilings of this place that houses some of the most extraordinary art pieces of all time. Truly, everyone knows these pieces: Degas, Van Gogh, Monet, Manet, Renoir, Gauguin.

It feels like walking into a church. I am reverent.

'I don't know where to go first,' I say.

Delphine moves around the space with confidence – she knows where to point me so I can find specific paintings I want to see. We glide about together, moving around the other museum-goers and their many languages and interests and so many people taking photos. I take photos.

There is a special exhibition called *Renoir père et fils. Peinture et cinéma.*

There's Pierre-August Renoir, the Impressionist painter.

Then his son, Jean Renoir, the cinematographer.

'I didn't know they were related,' I say. 'I suppose I should have worked it out.'

The idyllic country scenes in the movies and the paintings make me long for springtime and for the creek back home. It is magical and romantic – full of light and whimsy.

‘Do you paint?’ I ask Delphine. Perhaps art is passed down within families.

‘No, no,’ she says. ‘Just piano. And even then …’ She stifles something of a sigh.

I want to know more about this girl.

Here, in front of Pierre-August’s paintings, I realise where the spark for my daydreams may have originated. The white dresses on the girls and women in his paintings. The dappled light – *how does he make that effect?* I wonder, and get up as close as I can.

But Delphine’s reaction isn’t the same as mine. Her nose goes into the air as she observes the artwork. ‘All these paintings, all these artworks. Made by men looking at women,’ she says. ‘The women aren’t involved; they’re just for looking at.’

I’m not sure how to respond. It wasn’t my reaction – but I feel like maybe there is something, some kind of truth, nudging me. Her comment makes me think about Crow. Delphine obviously isn’t waiting for a response though, and we walk on, leaving *père* and *fils* behind, and I think I’m finally starting to understand the meaning of the ‘male gaze’.

We see Degas’s ballerinas. The colours and the brushstrokes are so familiar, but the full excited feeling inside me just grows and bubbles as we walk around the gallery. Cézanne, Gauguin, Manet and Monet and Van Gogh too.

‘I’ve seen paintings like these before,’ I say. ‘Exhibitions in Melbourne, you know.’

But I am looking at them with a new eye, somehow. Delphine’s criticism is astute, and it’s woken something up inside my brain. We look at Toulouse-Lautrec's pencil and oil and pastel sketches of Moulin Rouge dancers and women in the brothels.

'It makes you think about the lives lived and exploited, doesn't it?' I say.

'Oh yes, absolutely,' says Delphine. 'These pictures are both sexy and grotesque.'

What was he trying to tell us with this work, and how should we feel about it? Like Delphine, I feel conflicted. But maybe in a good way. A way that will affect how I approach my own art. Why this piece? What's my perspective? My bias? What am I trying to say?

'Thank you,' I say to Delphine. 'Thank you so much for bringing me here.'

'It's no problem,' she replies lightly.

But I'm actually worried that I might start to cry. My mind is spinning, my world is expanding – how could I have considered leaving and going back to the place I've always known like the back of my hand?

I feel my sense of adventure and quest for beauty revived. As we return home, even Belleville doesn't seem so ugly. It feels familiar, like the way people become better looking over time, as you get to know them.

Still, I plan to have a big cry in bed tonight, a big cry of relief and of exhaustion and of being overwhelmed with how lucky I am and how beautiful things can be.

I think I'm beginning to love this real version of Paris that I'm slowly getting to know. Or at least, I am starting to understand it better.

13

I begin to enjoy school as I immerse myself in the projects and challenges of my *Arts Plastiques* classes. They are like a soothing balm four times a week. Even though the words are foreign, I speak the language of pencil (*le crayon*), paintbrush (*le pinceau*) and canvas (*la toile*).

At school people are rough and loud – the voices hammer and echo off the concrete walls of the soulless courtyard when we stand around on break, shoving our hands into the pockets of our jackets.

Léa turns out to be really funny, and she is unstoppable with her eagerness to speak English with me, even though I still feel frustrated wanting to speak French. I have this idea that by speaking French I will become French – I will become sophisticated and worldly and an object of romance … but Léa wants to speak English. People ask her to ask me questions, and we all get to know each other in translation. I love listening to the way she makes mistakes.

I'm not sure it's equally as endearing when I make errors in French, though perhaps them laughing and correcting me isn't a reason to stop trying. But it does stop me trying.

But the atelier! In between classes I can go there and work on a drawing or look through the paints to make plans. There are often people around, but everyone is busy, and it feels like a productive but calm place to be.

The hours of school here are so different to back home. Sometimes I don't start until 10 am, but other times I have to get up early and go to school in the dim morning light for an 8.30 am class. I'll have an hour of *Histoire-Géo* and then have two hours free before Maths. Then the canteen for lunch.

Sometimes Léa drags me out to a café with one or more of her friends, where we sit shivering while they have coffee and smoke cigarettes, and I just hope no-one notices that I don't order anything.

In French *un café* is a coffee. *Un café* is also a café, like the coffee shop. Context is everything.

One afternoon we are in the café with a café, the sky icy blue above us. I'm wearing an oversized scarf I'd found at an op shop back home, and feel so much like I belong that I accidentally echo Léa's order of '*un petit café*' without thinking. Léa is texting her boyfriend, and I am assuming a confident air while doodling in my sketchbook to pass the time – when who should come sauntering along the road but Olivier, alongside Amandine, and *they sit down at the table right next to us.*

I (privately) swoon. A magnificent *oh là là* rolls off his tongue, and it doesn't sound affected or put on. I have an image of myself at some point in my Parisian future – my perfect hair, perfectly red-painted lips: *oh là là* – flitting off in a cloud of Chanel towards the metro.

Olivier lights his cigarette like he should be advertising them. He catches me looking at him (argh!), so I have to speak.

'Hi,' I say.

'Hi, Sofie,' he says. He turns his head to blow smoke away.

And, because I don't quite know how to continue the conversation, I slowly bring my tiny coffee cup to my mouth, but hesitate before sipping, self-consciously. I look at Olivier, my mind flicking over and over with possible questions and not landing on any.

I wet my lips again with coffee. It tastes bitter, but leaves a somehow-sweet flavour.

A waiter comes over and greets Olivier with enthusiasm, shaking his hand – '*Quoi de neuf?*' What's new? – and starts a conversation that I can't follow, just a few words snatched here and there.

I pull my attention away, to see Amandine leafing casually through my sketchbook, although when she notices me looking, she places it quickly back on my table. I pretend not to mind that she was peeping.

'Have you thought about your piece for the exhibition yet, Amandine?' I know already that Amandine is interested in sculpture and Cubism and using oversized house-painting brushes in her work. Véronique would, I'm sure, want me to take note of the freedom of Amandine's lines.

'Not yet,' she says, taking a cigarette and offering me one. I shake my head.

Suddenly Léa lurches forward, reaching out to touch Amandine on the arm and speaking in a rush. Her words are so fast that I can't make out their meaning, but it's clearly an important piece of news. Amandine leans forward too and they mutter between themselves. But it's not rude, somehow, and I just try to assume a detached air of confidence and ennui. The conversation will come back around again.

Olivier seems happy to sit and smoke; he seems comfortable with not being an active part of a conversation. I relax into my chair and let the girls' chatter flow around me. I pretend (with flair) that I too am comfortable not being an active part of a conversation. Really, it's just that I understand about fifty per cent of what is going on.

There are old men garbling at the next table, and the waiters are having a chat by the door, and it all washes through my ears as though I am underwater. I spot an elderly lady browsing over some endives at the fruit and vegetable shop across the road. Just one week ago I hadn't even known what an endive was. But then Claudette served up an endive salad (I'm starting to get used to having dinner at 9 pm now – it's very weird and wonderful), and the flavour was so new on my tongue that I wanted to spit it out. But when the meal was over, I had somehow grown to enjoy the fresh peppery taste.

'Do you have a piece of paper?' asks Olivier. There's laughter in him, making his body looser, and I feel myself growing excited and – uh oh – a bit of *silliness* coming on. Crow and I are often silly, though less and less as we get older. I miss it.

He takes the piece of paper and hunches his shoulders over it, hiding it from us as he draws. I both want to watch his hands and to be surprised with what he comes up with.

After a few minutes he makes a fold in the paper, lifts his head up – his brown eyes lovely and dark and laughing – and hands it to Amandine. The fold covers nearly all of his picture, just some lines spearing below the fold to show where his beginning ends.

'It is *le cadavre exquis* – the exquisite corpse game,' Olivier explains to me, while Amandine starts sketching on to the paper, a small private smile on her face. 'Each person just has a tiny hint to what might come next.'

I know this game. Crow and I played it often as children, mostly with silly stories. You write a line or two, leave a hint word or two showing, and then someone else continues the tale. We would cry with laughter at the nonsense we came up with. Like the story that began with a demure little girl called Crow who liked to eat the souls of racists, visited Paris with a fox, brought down civilisations using only an HB pencil, and wound up queen of the garbage dump with a teapot for a crown.

The page is handed to me. Amandine passes me a pen and I admire (and envy!) her perfect fingernails for just a moment, before turning my attention to the task.

I assume my bit is the belly. Olivier took the head, Amandine probably the shoulders. So I've got the guts, and I feel pressure to make it fascinating. I want to be sure to elevate what's come before. How do I be both funny and talented? Amandine's clues for me are two thick, rough points peeking from beneath the fold. I draw a round, fluffy tummy – I'm panicking because I started drawing before I thought about it.

'And I'm the feet?' Léa asks as I hand her the paper. She hardly pauses before she begins to draw. She finishes the final segment by swiping her pen across the paper at the bottom with a flourish. 'And this is why I don't take *les Arts Plastiques*!' she says, laughing.

Olivier takes the paper and unfolds it, taking time to look at it himself, before turning it around. His eyes dart across the page, lingering on one part, then the next, then scanning the whole. 'Thank you, everyone, and congratulations on a magnificent work,' he says, laughing.

'*Fais voir?*' I say. I've learned this means 'Let me see'.

'This is too funny,' says Amandine in her becoming-familiar monotone, letting the piece of paper drop back to the table.

I am happy our creation is more funny than monstrous. I would not call it exquisite, but Frankenstein would feel jealous at how well our corpse goes together. The head of a beautiful woman, her eyes closed, a crown of flowers, and narrow, naked shoulders leading down to a feathered torso – maybe bird-like? A prehistoric bird chest with jagged wings stretching out. My little chubby possum tummy, with its brush tail. Léa's contribution is sexy lady legs and a pair of fabulous 1970s platform shoes.

When I smile over at Olivier, he smiles back and winks quickly. Sometimes a wink can seem threatening, but this is conspiratorial, like we are somehow in it together. But what is *it*? I feel *seen* by him. I feel beautiful when he looks at me.

I haven't ever felt like this. I feel obsessed with his face. Could he look at me the same way? He *has* to! How is a crush supposed to feel? I feel crushed – heavy with expectation and dizzy with fighting against gravity. I feel magnetised.

14

A few days later, my *Arts Plastiques* class meets on the forecourt of the Centre Pompidou for an on-the-ground art lesson after school. I've got my sketchbook, my fine-liners and my pencils. I don't quite have a handle on keeping my crush under control.

Olivier is sitting on a step, reading a book called *L'Être et le Néant – Being and Nothingness*. It has a black and white photograph of a man on the back cover.

'I never knew that Jean-Paul Sartre had a lazy eye,' I say, in English.

He looks up from the page, with a quizzical glance, and I smile at him. He smiles back and I bloom a little inside.

Véronique leads us into the gallery, past Chagalls and Kandinskys and even Duchamps, to a painting of a woman in a green dress. She gives us our day's lesson – to create an art deco portrait in the style of Tamara de Lempicka. Then she sets us working with a wave of her hand.

I settle onto a bench and start sketching. I usually draw in my natural, preferred style, but it is good and challenging to try to improve my technique, and to imitate another artist's style. The women in De Lempicka's pieces have the most wonderful eyes. I am quickly absorbed. I only half see Olivier flick his curls away and barely notice his cheekbone when he does so.

My phone vibrates with a message and I swipe it open without putting down my pencil.

Are you OK? It's from Mum. Then another: *Reply to this RIGHT AWAY.*

I stare for a bit and try to think of reasons I might not be okay, and why she needs to know so urgently. It's 2 am at home.

I'm ok, I type. *Why? What are you doing up?*

While I watch the three dots go, another message beeps. It's Crow. *Shit Sof, tell me you're ok!* There is a link as well.

As I click it, Mum's reply comes through: *Explosion in Paris near Eiffel Tower.*

I sit very still, but a strange feeling floods through me. It is fear, as though any second now this street, this building, this room, this me could be blown to smithereens. But it is also a kind of excitement, which makes me feel terrible.

I quickly text Mum back: *I'm fine. With my Art class.*

Then I message Crow: *I'm fine! We didn't even know!*

I wait for her link to load, look around at the group – heads bowed over drawings, noses almost pressed to paper to capture details. Olivier rubs his thumb along a line of charcoal, smudging it just a touch.

Just a touch. Of his thumb.

But – the message. The disaster. The fear …

The news article is short. Reports of an explosion in the Paris metro. All trains stopped.

'Something exploded,' I say out loud, and somehow it comes out in French. I don't quite believe it myself. I don't feel qualified to share this news.

A few people raise their heads and look at me. I hold up my phone, as if presenting evidence, and the class begins to murmur. One by one, each person picks up their phone.

'*Mais jen'y crois pas …*'

'*Oh là là …*'

Véronique is stern. 'Please feel free to go home. If for any reason you can't get home, come back here until it's safe to do so.'

Home – both Melbourne home and Belleville home – feels very far away and if I could teleport to either one of them right now I would.

Extra museum security guards have appeared, seemingly from nowhere, and are silently waving people towards the exits. Everyone feeds each other with little bits of information as we gather our things and leave:

It was a car bomb. They'd shot a suspect dead.

Actually, there was an accidental fire.

No, it really was a bomb.

It's so hard to know what's real news.

What is real is the metro is closed down. No trains home.

I try to call Claudette, but the coverage seems to be jammed. I can't connect.

Now it isn't a bomb at all, but the threat of gas released in the metro.

It is the yellow vests, it is just a train strike, it is terrorists.

I want to panic. But I also want to keep my shit together. This is just another test in the series of tests as part of the rather big experiment of Sofie Visits Another Country All On Her Own.

'Can I walk you home?' asks Olivier.

His offer feels entirely overwhelming. But I play it cool. I wave a hand at him, doing my best Hana. 'No, I'll be fine.'

'Are you sure?' He looks concerned, peering at me from behind his curly brown hair that is falling artfully across his face. I'm not so scared that I am beyond noticing things like this. I draw a lock of his hair in my mind.

'I can get a *Vélib*,' I explain. The *Vélib* is the street bike thing I've not actually used before, but it doesn't look too hard to work out. You just have to have a credit card, and Mum gave me one to use in emergencies. And if this isn't an emergency, then I don't know what is!

But there are no bikes left when we get there. I feel wobbly. *Please stay with me*, I think. *Please offer again to walk me home.*

'Come on,' Olivier says. 'I'll walk you home.'

My heart! It smashes against my breastbone.

We walk along streets and people hurry alongside us. No-one really looks at each other. A few people seem alarmed, but most are just getting on with their walk home. I wonder if we are in this together or if everyone is suspicious of one other.

It seems strange to have a normal conversation in such an abnormal situation. But what else is there to do? Conversation will keep us anchored in reality.

'Are you enjoying your exchange?' Olivier asks.

'I am. I've dreamed about coming to Paris for a long time.' He nods, smiles, and so I go on. 'I miss home though. My family. They're all going to our holiday house this weekend. It's my grandfather's house, really. They'll take him down there to give him a break from the nursing home. It's a good place for drawing – lots of trees and details for landscapes.'

'Véronique says trees are good practice for learning to draw with flow,' he says. 'There are no straight lines in nature.'

'That's true. I hadn't thought about it like that. I've always found it hard to capture nature in my drawings. It's a constant challenge for me.'

'I like the beach,' says Olivier. 'But not really the countryside. My—'

He is interrupted by a loud bang. My stomach lurches with instant fear. I don't even have time to react before he grabs my arm and we stumble away from the side of the road.

When we look around, unblown-up, we figure out the bang was from a car driving over a plastic bag, causing it to pop. That was all it was. Relief comes out of me in the form of one big breath.

'This isn't right,' Olivier says. 'We aren't supposed to live like this.'

'But there's nothing we can do.' (There is definitely nothing I can do. He is still holding my arm. I'm amazed my feet are still on the ground.)

I can tell that the bang frightened him. Not just

surprised him, but frightened him. Seeing Olivier scared makes him less dream, more human person, and this is where I pinpoint my crush blowing out into Real Feelings. I hug his arm and it feels appropriate, and not out of the ordinary.

We walk along the Rue Vieille du Temple with our arms linked – cars and taxis are banked up along it, their headlights and tail-lights illuminating the narrow road and the brown-grey stone buildings – and we talk. And we step up and down and on and off the curb to dodge worried-looking people.

'*Putain de merde*, I am so angry.'

Olivier makes me think of Crow. She would be angry too.

'But what can you do about it?' I ask him again.

Olivier bristles. 'I can't do anything about it. Nobody can. We have a weak government. They need to protect people, make decisions for peace. That is democracy.' He speaks so fiercely I get a fright. I haven't heard him talk like this before. I haven't heard him care so much. 'That is our right.'

I care too. When we talk about privilege and war and climate change, I feel fear and worry and hope and confusion … but it's all so much I don't know what to do about it or even what to say.

When Crow is angry, she knows exactly what she wants to say. 'And you know it's America's capitalist greed that's caused all this unrest in the Middle East and inflamed racial and religious tensions all around the world. We're victims!' she'd said once. And she wrote an essay that won two prizes and delivered a speech with a snarl on her face. Even the teachers are frightened of her.

The thing is, if a sixteen-year-old girl like Crow can see these things, then surely the people in charge can see them too? I get that power is complicated, but I can't do anything about anything. *Someone* in charge has to though.

At least Olivier still has his arm entwined with mine. We walk in silence for a little bit as the neat stone buildings give way to the slightly grubby shopfronts that mark the 11th and then the 20th arrondissements.

'Did you know that when World War II broke out, they closed the museums in Paris and took the art to safe places for storage?' I say.

'But of course,' he replies.

I try to think of something else interesting. 'It's a cold night to walk the streets of Paris. I'm sorry.'

'Don't be sorry.' And just like that, he lets go of my arm. But before I can even feel disappointed, his fingers curl into mine and we are holding hands.

I can't bear to look at him because the smile on my face is too large.

From a horrible situation – we still don't know what has happened – I can't help but feel a most incredible thing is blossoming.

15

The morning after the metro closure and the long walk home, some people from school ask me to go to the movies with them. Well, Léa does: 'We're going to the cinema on Friday. Do you want to come?'

Claudette seems a bit annoyed when I ask her permission to go. '*Bah, oui, bien sûr.*' Then, as an afterthought: 'But come home by eleven. And take the metro. Don't walk. Delphine says you walk everywhere.'

'I like walking.' I also like the expression *bah, oui*. It makes me think of Crow rolling her eyes, going *well, derrrrr.*

'Are you afraid of the metro since … what happened?' Claudette asks.

I shake my head, trying to suppress a smile as I remember my walk with Olivier. 'No.'

'Good.'

I'd noticed little, curious things about the city as we'd walked home that night – even with the distraction of the hand-holding. Tiny fragments. Tiny beautifuls.

After I'd made it home that night, I'd made notes for a Panic Map, with landmarks showing where the plastic bag had popped; where I heard a dog bark; and where I saw two homeless people lying over the metro grates that would usually offer warmth because of the trains running underneath, but which would remain cold that night.

As I sketched, the group message chat with the other exchange students who lived outside of Paris lit up with messages *ping ping ping ping*. They wanted to know what it had been like when the trains went down and the city was in momentary panic. I didn't tell them about the hand-holding (even though I haven't stopped thinking about it and have taken to entwining my fingers to remind me how it had felt when Olivier's fingers had fitted in with mine) – but I did tell them about the walk across the city.

That night, when we were a bit more than halfway home, the network must have unjammed because our phones came alive again, messages pinging through – Olivier and I had to drop each other's hands to check our phones – and within a minute Claudette had called me.

'Sofie, where are you?' she asked in English, her voice worried.

I told her I was with a friend and we were coming up the Rue de Belleville, and she made Delphine run down and meet us.

'Are you all right?' Delphine asked me, the reflective panels on her running shoes glinting in the streetlight. '*Bonsoir*,' she said politely to Olivier, and they gave *les bises*.

'*Salut, Delphine*,' Oliver said, and I hadn't realised they knew each other. But neither of their tones were super warm. I glanced from one to the other, trying to work them out.

Back at the house, Claudette and Léon were surprised to see Olivier with me, but greeted him warmly and explained they were friends with his parents. Small world. Claudette offered for Olivier to stay and have dinner with us because it was getting late and who knew how long it would take him to get home.

'Thank you very much,' he said politely. 'My father has already sent a car.'

I felt like a tightly strung harp. Like I was taking up all the room or, at least, my feelings were. I felt like everyone could see me, could hear my heartstrings go *plink plink plink plink plink plink plink thrummmmmmmmmmm.*

Also – his father was sending a car? Even my harp-self realised this wasn't an ordinary thing. Who *was* he?

Olivier hadn't seemed fazed or different as he chatted with Claudette and Léon. There wasn't a skerrick of the frightened Olivier I'd glimpsed on our walk home, and soon he had a message to say his car was waiting. We all said *bonsoir* politely, and I waved him goodbye in the hall. His return wave from the elevator had me smiling to myself as I closed the door.

Back in the apartment, Claudette and Léon looked at me with relief. I guess it would be quite terrible if I were damaged while I was in their care.

'I'll make us a tisane,' said Delphine, and we all sat around the television in the living room, the news on while we murmured theories to each other. Despite the seriousness of the situation, I still found space to be amused at how all French news hosts seem to look exactly the same.

'Ah, an update,' said Léon, and he jumped up to stand closer to the television, to hear better.

I felt drained, but I leaned forwards to concentrate. The French speak so fast.

'What a relief,' said Claudette.

Delphine repeated the news, for my benefit. It turned out it wasn't a bomb, but a mechanical failure resulting in an explosion in the metro. They are redoing a bunch of stations, and it had just been one of those unfortunate workplace accidents.

Bonne nuit.

I had hoped Olivier might be in the group going to the movies on Friday, but it seems like this is more the music crowd.

As well as Léa and Amandine, there's Victor-with-the-shaved-head and a girl called Maleeka I haven't met before. We go to see a Hollywood blockbuster and they buy my ticket for me. Even though the cinema could be a Hoyts back home, with the same posters and the smell of popcorn, it does feel different. Special, in a way, though I feel a bit silly for thinking so. The others all chatter in fast French as we find our seats. I catch phrases here and there.

The movie starts and a Big Hollywood Star delivers his first line … and it's not him! It's an entirely different voice and it's entirely in French. It's so weird!

'*Eh!*' Léa, sitting next to me, notices my surprise and laughs. 'In France you can choose *VO*, which is *version originale*—'

'This is dubbed,' explains Amandine in a whisper, sitting on my other side. 'But it's better like this for us. Does it bother you?'

'*Je m'en fiche*,' I say. It is a new phrase I've learned: 'I don't give a damn.' I even attempt a little shrug.

They laugh, which was my intention. I suppose I am basically French now. And my confidence pushes me to steal a handful of popcorn right out of Léa's bag without asking. She just tilts it in my direction for easier access.

'*Merci*.' I'm starting to feel comfortable and I can't believe how happy it makes me.

I understand about half of the film, but can fill in the blanks by the Very Dramatic acting and explosions. It's not really my kind of thing. *Je m'en fiche.* I am just happy to be included. It is nice to sit in the dark with new friends and handfuls of popcorn taken in turn.

Out on the street, it has snowed! And it's still snowing. The footpath is wet and slushy, but snow is piling up around trees and shrubs in the park opposite in a picturesque way.

My friends all light up cigarettes and casually blow smoke, while I try to act cool about it. Back home I know only a handful of people my age who smoke. Some people would have a ciggie at parties but it isn't like this.

I learn a new word: *une clope*. It means cigarette, but in slang! Like a ciggie. I still don't want to smoke them, but I am happy to know the word.

I look it up later on the internet and apparently 40 per cent of French teenagers smoke. That's unreal! *C'est dingue!*

'You don't smoke?' asks Victor, who I've figured out now is the *petit-ami* of Amandine.

I shake my head.

'I'll probably stop when I'm thirty,' explains Maleeka. 'Maybe.'

Even though I am basically French now – with my French friends and my French-dubbed movie – the slang, like the smoking, is still impossible to understand. Impossible!

'*Allez! On va faire un MacDo,*' says Victor.

And lo, I am inducted into what I learn is a popular pastime of French teenagers. It's basically French for 'Let's go on a Macca's run'.

Parts of the footpath are slick with ice, and I tread carefully. As we walk, Maleeka tells a dramatic story, at such a speed I decide to just enjoy the sound of her voice and the expression on her face. The others laugh, gasp and add shocked '*Mais, non!*' from time to time.

'*... un truc d'ouf!*' she finishes.

This is one expression Delphine had explained to me: '*Truc* equals thing. You can use this when you've forgotten the word for something or if you're not being specific. But *ouf*' – she laughed – 'it's *fou,* the word for crazy, in reverse. You swap the syllables, so the word goes upside down. In a sense.'

That's when I finally understood *verlan*, the slang word for French slang. It's the word *l'envers* – meaning back to front – but the word itself is turned upside down and inverted. *Ver-lan. L'en-vers.*

While my brain is buzzing, I try to tell the group – in my little French, my broken Franglais – about how I am going to be an artist. *Je voudrais être artiste.* At first I'm not sure whether I should reveal my Instagram account (130 new followers since I arrived in France!) but I cross my fingers and my toes that they like me and the stuff I've been posting.

We follow each other online.

At McDonald's, over *un Big Mac avec des frites*, I learn a little more about their home lives, their backgrounds. They all live around me – some within the *périphérique* and some just on the other side. They are dance students, musicians, writers in training.

'My cousin takes piano with Delphine Durant,' says Hassim. 'He said she's hyper-intelligent, but a bit of a rabbit joy.'

'A what?' I ask.

Un rabat-joie. We google it. Buzzkill.

I kind of agree, but also not really. Delphine is always so busy and rushing around. I don't think someone so interested in something can be a buzzkill. Delphine is always neat, in spite of her hurry, so put together. I can easily imagine her at home in a designer house, playing a piano.

It is 10 pm when we head home. If it was just me, I would walk, but we're all going in pretty much the same direction, so I get the metro with them.

I feel part of things. It is as if I could see us all from above. A group of youths, *jeunes*, *ados*. All swiping our Navigos, *boop boop*, and Maleeka jumping casually over the turnstile. Farewelling each other with, '*À la prochaine!*' and '*Salut!*' '*Salut!*'

Back at the apartment I remember to shake the snow off my coat before I go inside. Imagine being the kind of person who has to shake snow off their clothes! Funny how it's these small things that really remind me I am in another country. I send Crow a message: *I am having a grand adventure.*

While I lie in bed that night, my brain is exhausted but also happy. I did it. Made conversation. Watched a movie in French. Had a lot of fun.

I text Mum about my night, and she replies right away, all *but I thought we weren't allowed to see new movies without each other.* So I send back an eyeroll emoji.

I sit and look out the window and think about the day. There's a person out there walking a dog, and a couple of cars go past.

I have friends here. I can make people laugh on purpose while speaking a foreign language. I have held hands with a beautiful French boy. I am building a life in Paris.

If my night out was an artwork it would be colourful and Cubist.

16

Léon has an art show coming up and there is a *vernissage* planned. I learn right away that this means an 'opening night'.

'Are you coming to the *vernissage*?' Léon asks, the morning before.

Like there's any way he can keep me away! 'Yes, of course,' I say.

I will be an insider. I will practically be family at this art show opening night. An art show in Paris! I have a moment where I imagine Léon asking if I want to take a wall and show my own pieces. But it's just a moment, and I'm glad I can pull myself back in before that little dream gets too out of control.

He picks up his keys from the hall table and pauses. 'Would you like to come with us to my studio and help me make my final selections?'

'*Oui, merci!*'

The key to Léon's atelier is big, black and ornate – like it's out of Harry Potter or *Coraline* or something. I immediately want to hold it, draw it, open some magic door with it.

We go up flights of stairs. Flights and flights. 'Space is hard to find,' Léon says as we climb. 'But ten years ago we found this little *chambre de bonne* and it's worked very well.'

It's on the very top floor. 'So what do you think?' he asks.

I don't say anything for a moment as I look around. 'It's … small,' I say eventually, because it's true and because I somehow can't stop myself.

'These apartments were traditionally maid's quarters,' explains Claudette.

There's a window recessed into the wall, and I open it. I lean against the iron railing, taking in the view of the city across rooftops and skyline and even the Eiffel Tower.

Now this is what I had imagined!

Léon's work is scary. I had seen it online, of course, but that was before I came here and met him. Now I'm finding it hard to reconcile the quiet, friendly man with this harsh and grotesque work. It's modern. Like Jackson Pollock meets Franz Kline via Kandinsky.

'Expressionist?' I ask.

He nods, smiles, gestures 'so-so' with his hand.

Some of the canvases are small. But some are as tall as me, and thinking of the climb we just made, I wonder out loud: 'How will you get the paintings out?'

Léon's looking intently through the canvases, moving some here and others there.

'It's common for removalists to bring a big lift,' says Claudette. 'We will move the paintings out through the window.'

Amazing. I look out again, lean over the iron railing as

far as I dare, and imagine the lift – in my mind it's something like a cherry picker – coming all the way up here.

While Léon waits for the truck and the lift that will bring his artwork safely to the ground, Claudette says, 'Sofie, come and help me with the wine.'

I follow her, the heels of her sensible stair-climbing shoes tapping as we descend again. We get to the ground floor, but it turns out we've got to go further.

We go through a half-sized door where we have to duck our heads, and into a basement where the floor isn't floor at all but packed earth. It smells like the goldmine tour at Sovereign Hill.

'This is our *cave*,' Claudette explains, as we walk down a narrow corridor.

'*Cave?*' I ask. (It's pronounced like 'cahve'.)

She stops by a wooden door that wouldn't be out of place in a barn, and uses a modern little key in a modern-looking deadlock. It's a small room – maybe two metres deep – with big industrial shelving filled with bottles and bottles of wine.

Claudette selects wine and puts it into boxes by the door. 'I don't know if we need glasses,' she muses. Boxes of wine glasses are packed neatly against one wall.

There are canvases down here too, covered in tarpaulins.

'These are old pieces,' Claudette tells me. 'Léon's *folies*.' She looks at the boxes she's arranged, all neat and ready for the *vernissage*. 'Okay. Ready?' And it's time for the stairs again.

After the small moving van – *camionette* – tootles off around the corner carrying the art pieces to the gallery,

Claudette and Léon say they want to take me to Père Lachaise Cemetery. I wonder briefly if they're making sure to tick off 'include your exchange student in your daily life' and 'engage your exchange student in cultural activities of your area' from the organisation's *famille d'accueil*, aka, the host family checklist.

Once we arrive, we stand in front of the map that shows the main attractions of the cemetery and marks the routes to find where the people of note are buried. For a cemetery, this place is busy, and I spot at least five people moving along the paths. I find I don't feel frightened or strange being here among all these slumbering souls.

I sit down on a stone bench and roughly sketch the tomb of Oscar Wilde before walking around to study the inscription and run my fingers across the array of lipstick kisses.

Claudette walks up the path, reading headstones. Her grey coat falls to her ankles and is cinched at the waist with a tailored belt like a movie star. She's dried her hair sleek and let it hang straight to her shoulders instead of clipping it back with a large silver hair clasp like usual. I covet her casual weekend glamour just as much as her weekday chic.

I up my pace to catch her and Léon.

Further on, there is a clear patch of grass and a great expanse of stone wall. A plaque reads, in gold lettering: *'AUX MORTS DE LA COMMUNE 21-28 MAI 1871'*. One hundred and forty-seven communards were shot here during the Paris Commune.

I make a note to google the Paris Commune because I can't remember why they killed these people. I place my hands flat against the wall and lean into it (looking around first to make sure no-one sees), trying to feel the history.

We wander down the paths, and I tiptoe around broken headstones and polished ones, admire the really ornate ones and hypothesise about the ones that look like shrines or confessionals. Some headstones are completely grown over with ivy and creeping plants.

We say little to one another. Murmur '*regarde*' (look) and point out things. It's peaceful here.

I am fascinated by the twisted grotesque statues, which stand in memory of those who lost their lives in the Holocaust. They look like skeletons, carrying one another. It's moving, but repulsive. There is one that looks like an enormous alien baby carved smooth out of a knobbly hunk of stone. They make me think about Léon's paintings.

We visit Jim Morrison, who my dad loves. Both Claudette and Léon are cynical about Jim's grave and mutter rude things about all the tourists who come to obsess over a singer. Though after we walk on, I can hear Léon humming 'Light My Fire' under his breath.

I might have walked through the Melbourne Cemetery once or twice to get to the city, but never ambled through for pleasure. But it turns out it is a pleasure – the grey and brown grimness, the dampness of the path underneath. It is the same kind of beauty I feel watching a sad film, or staring at the paintings of Klimt or Picasso's blue period.

It ends up being such a fascinating, surprising day, and even while it's happening, I think, *This is a milestone moment.* Claudette suggests a meal at *un p'tit resto* that they love not too far from Père Lachaise. Even Delphine agrees to meet us there, turning up from wherever she's been (I would love to know) with her face flushed, her hair messily plaited into a braid that hangs over one shoulder.

I don't catch everything Léon says as she arrives – kissing each of us in turn, *bisous bisous* – but I hear words about a secret boyfriend or something.

'Just stop, *papa*,' she says, and I recognise the tone in her voice. Hana uses the same one when she's a moment away from storming out during a conversation with Dad about her 'evil corporate job'.

'So how did you meet?' I ask my host parents. We sit on the restaurant terrace, a gas heater in the awning above us bathing us in a hot glow. I had practised this question, among others, because Hana says it's important to be interested. *Interested people are interesting*, she says.

Claudette's mouth has a bit of an unreadable quality about it, thin lips and slight wrinkles – I suppose from pursing them to pronounce all those pursed-lip French 'u' words, like *dessus*, *sur* and *sucre*.

'We were at university together.' (There's that 'u' sound again, *u-niversité*). 'At the École des Beaux-Arts.'

'How romantic!' I say.

Not going to lie, I get an instant daydream:

Me and Olivier, university students together at the École des Beaux-Arts, living in a little flat (it looks suspiciously like Léon's atelier, if I'm honest). It has a mattress on the floor with expensive-but-crumpled sheets and a stack of clothbound, hardback books.

The waiter places a silver bowl on our table, piled with

ice, and resting atop the ice are freshly shucked oysters. I hadn't even heard them order!

Delphine waves her hand. 'I'm not eating those,' she says.

Claudette looks at me. 'My daughter is going to be a vegetarian now.' Her tone sounds like it is encouraging me to disapprove.

I look quickly at Delphine, but she is checking her phone, her eyebrows furrowed as she taps out a message.

I watch as Léon takes his tiny fork and gently prods at the little slimy thing. He brings the shell up and, with an almost inaudible slurp, tips the oyster into his mouth. Claudette does the same.

Delphine takes a drink of water and looks bored. (She looks like she's in an advertisement for water or a café or a hair salon maybe.) I feel an urge to draw her.

'And now you work in a gallery,' I say. Claudette nods. 'And Léon, you paint.'

I pick up an oyster and try to copy them. The oyster feels like slippery jelly under my fork.

'Yes, that's right,' says Léon. 'And I teach, a little.'

I take the plunge. It is like taking a mouthful of seawater. *Are you supposed to chew it?!* I feel panicked and just force myself to swallow it whole. It's not bad, but a thoroughly new sensation. I know that I will recall this flavour and this moment, with its very strange and all-powerful joy, well into my future.

A surprise wind blows some rogue winter leaves along the street.

'*On est bien là*,' says Léon, leaning back in his chair. How nice is this.

17

The afternoon of the *vernissage*, Delphine and I are roped into helping. We go to a particular bakery, as instructed by Léon, to collect some tiny delicious-looking cakes, and then we go to another bakery and buy a cloth bag filled with baguettes.

I've come to learn that most people here have their favourite shop for each specific thing. They get their fish here, their cheese here, their meat here. I love the sense of neighbourhood. I draw all of Claudette and Léon's shops in a row and label them with the products they sell:

Filets d'agneau

Saumon fumé

Rocamadour (fromage de chèvre)

Baguette tradition

Petits-fours

'This part of the *vernissage* is important,' Delphine explains. 'Papa likes to do it house-made. He doesn't want to pay a caterer.'

'Homemade,' I correct her, gently, without thinking.

She doesn't pause. 'Homemade,' she repeats. It doesn't

seem to bother her to make mistakes. Interesting.

'Is it still *fait à la maison* if we buy it all from the shops?' I ask as we walk back to the gallery, and even though I am being dead serious, Delphine laughs. Even her laugh is beautiful.

'This is true. But I think it will be okay.'

We find Léon standing by the car in front of the gallery. The cartons of wine from the *cave* are at his feet and a cigarette is between his teeth.

Claudette has agreed to stop by the *boucherie* on her way home from work and she arrives soon after we do, carrying salami, pâté, foie gras, nuts.

The gallery owners have decorated everything with plants and flowers – or maybe their gallery always looks like this – and the place is beautiful. It contrasts with the tone of the paintings, but somehow, the more I look at Léon's art in this context, the more sense it makes. I see elements of Munch, Kandinsky, Kirchner.

'Do you know the Australian painter John Brack?' I ask Léon as he passes by.

He stops. 'I do. Why?'

I point to one of his pieces, rendered in browns and yellows. 'This one reminds me a bit of Brack.'

Léon tilts his head while he considers it. 'Yes, yes, I can see how you see that.' He smiles warmly and moves away.

Delphine and I lay out the food and once we're done it looks extravagant. I feel a bit overwhelmed at how much food there is, while at the same time making a mental note of all the things I want to taste.

~

There is so much kissing. Whenever new people arrive we *mwah mwah, bisous bisous.*

Then there he is. Olivier.

He is easy and funny and oh so *charmant*. I'm watching him, so I see when he spots me, and my heart goes *eeeeeeeeeeeeeeeeeeeeeeeeee* when he makes his way straight over. He kisses me on the cheeks, *mwah mwah.*

'You're all covered in flour,' he says.

Mortifying! 'I am?' I twist to see what he's talking about while he laughs. Why didn't Delphine tell me?

He reaches out and dusts the flour off my dress with firm brushes of his hand. I'm in my black smock with the belt around it (it's become a uniform) but this time I'm wearing a long, pink silk scarf in my hair. He adjusts my scarf back into place carefully, and I don't think I'm imagining the way he lets it run through his fingers. This isn't the closest we've been – I mean, we held hands for an hour just the week before. But it feels more intimate and I can't explain why.

'I carried a bread bag,' I explain, feeling stupid.

Olivier smiles.

I smile.

I can't even understand what I'm feeling. Is this some kind of spontaneous social anxiety? Or is this how romance actually feels? It's as though I want to look at his face for days, examine the dark brown of his eyes and the perfect slope of his jawline. Enjoy the way that his eyebrow hairs go a bit skew-whiff above his nose, like they might one day join forces, but for now they just give him a rakish, unkempt kind of look. His skin is so beautiful I even forget about my pimples (in French they call them *boutons*, which is too cute a name for pimples, except that if Olivier had pimples, they would definitely be called *boutons*).

'You look beautiful,' he says.

I am stumped for a moment. 'Even with the flour?' I ask.

He laughs. 'Like a beautiful girl from the *boulangerie*.'

We look into each other's eyes. I've seen this in movies, but never realised that it is highly likely at least one of them is actually looking to try to work out what the other person is thinking. For example, I am thinking that I would like to kiss his face and not in the polite French greeting way. But maybe he's just thinking, *I am a polite person. Look at me making direct eye contact*. I will my eyes to explain that I think he is charming and I think he is beautiful and I think we should kiss each other on the face.

More people arrive, and Olivier and I are jostled away from one another. I don't mind. I figure he'll stick around for a little while – standing over there with those people *who look suspiciously like they could be his parents* – and staying away from him for a bit is a really handy way of playing it cool. I have zero chill.

Saying that, I like the way I can blend into the background. I watch everybody *faire la bise* and look at the art and explain things to one another and congratulate Léon on the show. He stands among the crowd in his peach shirt and his checked woollen pants, the perfect combination of shabby and chic.

I catch glimpses throughout the night of Olivier.

Olivier eating some salami.

Olivier looking at a painting.

Olivier running his hand through his curls.

Delphine comes and stands next to me. 'I cannot abide that man,' she says, with a tilt of her head towards a tall grey-haired man with a flowery silk scarf tied around his neck (who is talking to Olivier with a disgruntled look on his face).

'He's quite fancy,' I say, trying to sound neutral. Fancy people intrigue me, so I don't want to pass judgement just yet.

'He's a rich fool,' she replies. 'They all are.' She is muttering in French under her breath, something about *le privilège blanc*. Then she grabs a glass of wine from a passing tray and heads off towards the food, her voice dropping to a whisper as she goes: 'You know he's your boyfriend's father.'

'He's not my boyfriend,' I hiss back, but Delphine is gone. I am mortified but also elated she thinks Olivier could be my boyfriend. But I don't know how I feel about the rich fancy man being Olivier's dad.

Le privilège blanc. White privilege. Nearly all of the people at the *vernissage* are white. Wait. Okay, yes. Ninety-nine per cent of the guests are white. It feels weird, when out on the street – in Belleville, in my school, on the metro – the percentage is very different.

I am distracted then, trying to figure out how to say ninety-nine in French. Counting is hard. Ninety-nine. Okay, so that's *quatre vingt dix-neuf*. Four-twenty-nineteen. Sometimes I think French is a totally stupid language. But I feel pretty gleeful at being able to speak it better and better.

I catch snippets of the conversations going on around

me and I try to commit pieces of them to memory. Art, holidays, a grandmother who is hoarding her diamonds.

There is no need for daydreaming here. I am living some kind of dream life.

Delphine comes back, with a napkin holding fruit and nuts, and offers it to me.

When people speak with Delphine, she always introduces me and I say *bonjour* and *c'est un plaisir* and *ouais, c'est magnifique* (that is if they ask me about the work).

The paintings are hung without frames – big stretched canvases with their confronting scenes. The show is called *Quelque Chose Qui Cloche. There Is Something Wrong.*

'The paintings look good here,' I say.

She nods, but I don't think she's really listening. Everyone looks so effortlessly cool, so chic and Parisian, and this is exactly what I came to France for.

People speak English with me sometimes, but it feels conversational or cosmopolitan, and not like I am some stupid child who can't speak the language. Not once am I called *la petite Australienne.*

I am part of this scene. I am part of this.

18

By 10 pm people are leaving. It has been a long night at the *vernissage*, but it turns out the next part of the plan is a dinner at someone's house – a big, fancy Paris apartment.

'I'm not going to that fool's house,' Delphine says under her breath to me. Then to Claudette: '*Maman*, I'm going home to prepare for running club tomorrow morning. We're meeting early.'

'Will you go home too, Sofie?' Claudette asks.

I feel intensely disappointed. I definitely do not want to go home just yet. 'Um,' I say. And it must show on my face.

'You can stay, of course, Sofie. It's not a problem. Celebrate with us. We will go to Pierre and Louise's apartment for dinner.'

'Okay,' I say nonchalantly. But I'm thrilled on the inside! Then I realise who she means. Pierre the fool – as in Olivier's father! I thrill on the outside too – all the hairs on my arms stand on end.

'*D'accord. À demain, Sofie. Salut, maman, je t'aime.*' And with that, Delphine is off. There's something very funny about watching her speed off down the street – she's not running, on account of her fancy clothes and shoes, but she gives off a running vibe nonetheless.

'Should I collect the platters?' I ask.

Claudette shakes her head. Her mind is far away from packing up, I can tell. 'We will come by tomorrow and collect these things. Let's not think about it now. I must see if Léon is ready. Are you ready, Sofie?'

I have the strangest suspicion that Claudette is a little bit drunk. I haven't ever seen her have more than a glass or two of wine, but if I'm honest, everyone is getting rather rowdy. It feels kind of exciting.

We all troop out of the venue, Léon throwing *mercis* to the gallery owners and saying quietly to Claudette, 'Eight sales, *bof – c'est pas mal. C'est déjà pas mal.*' Not bad, not bad at all.

Bof. I plan to use this expression a lot. It's usually combined with the shrug, which I am already very good at. And you can even add the pursed lips action for extra flair. '*Bof, euhhhh, ppt.*' I make a mental note to write this down in my HOW TO BE FRENCH notes.

I stick close by Claudette as we move through the streetlamp-lit street, a clear sky above us and a freezing bite to the air. 'Where is the house? Is it far away?' I can't see Olivier, though I'm looking around for him. Surely he's coming home too.

'It's just straight ahead, and then around the corner. They have such a wonderful space. It used to belong to his grandmother. She knew Coco Chanel.'

There's a French word, *chamboulée*, which means turned upside down or all over the place. It expresses perfectly how

I feel right now. I am going to the house of a ridiculously chic woman (I had fawned over her camel-coloured coat earlier) and her husband, whose very grandmother knew Coco Chanel. *Sacrébleu!* I am going to *Olivier's house*!

The group arrives at the building. Someone enters the code and everyone starts to file through heavy black doors with a big brass handle. The front doors to apartments in Paris are magical things. I've drawn so many of them. They're so big and ornate they seem medieval or from a fairytale. This one is painted a sleek black, but I've seen others: blue, grey, the occasional pop of red. I always like to imagine what kind of lives go on behind these doors.

The air is cold and still. I can see my breath. A voice behind me says, 'Sofie, wait. I want to have a cigarette. Wait with me?' And Olivier, appearing from somewhere, catches me around the waist.

My friends have hugged me before, obviously. My sister has slung her arm around my waist my entire life, posing for photographs on holidays or standing united before our parents. I've kissed an uncountable amount of people since arriving in France. *Bisous bisous bisous bisous.*

But his arm around my waist is something else indeed.

'Do you want a cigarette?'

I shake my head.

'Little innocent,' he teases. He lets me go and leans against the building wall. His long legs are crossed over at the ankle and his body half-turned towards me. I am transfixed.

'What did you think of Léon's show?' I ask.

He nods, and I interpret it as thoughtful nodding.

'*Pas mal.* Interesting.' More nodding. More darkly intense staring. He turns his cigarette over and over in his fingers but doesn't light it. 'I don't think my father will buy anything, but yes, the work is not bad.'

I am a bit offended on Léon's behalf, even though I feel unsettled by his art or, at the very least, I don't fully understand it. But on the other hand, Léon had made a number of sales, and Delphine said Olivier's dad is a bit of a pompous dick anyway.

'It was a great party though.' Olivier smiles, puts the cigarette back in the packet. 'I think I'll smoke this later.'

With his arm tucked tight around me, I feel secure as we trip (in the cute, happy goat-stepping kind of way) towards the building. Olivier enters the code and holds the door open for me. As I walk through, he catches my shoulder, moves his hand to my neck, to my face. I feel his thumb rub gently – oh so gently – across my cheek.

This is happening. It is really happening. My breath catches, and I feel giddy and afraid and excited all at once.

He laughs lightly, and before I know it his lips press against mine. It is a sensation utterly unlike any other in my life. I move closer, raised up onto my tippy toes, to press into his lips a little harder. It feels soft and gentle and warm, and absolutely wonderful. His hand runs down across my shoulder blades and comes to rest in the small of my back. As the kiss ends and he pulls away, I already want to be back there. I know there and then that I will never forget the feeling or the flavour.

'*Allez, zou*,' he says quietly, pulling at my hand. And we go up the stairs.

Any other time I would have stopped to marvel at the staircase. Worn wooden steps curving up and up and around, with an iron-and-wood bannister. A view down to the black-and-white tiled floor in the entranceway where not a minute ago I was being kissed, I was kissing, I was kissed. (Who am I kidding – the staircase, the bannister, the black-and-white tiled floor all swirl and tie in to the moment.)

But mostly I am marvelling at something else: I know what someone else's lips feel like.

The rest of the night passes in a blur. The apartment is filled with fancy wooden furniture, and loud conversations and clinking and clanking of glasses and plates and knives and forks.

We eat green beans and carrots dripping with butter and some kind of juicy flavoursome meat with potatoes alongside it. Roasted garlic, served with the papery skins still on. There is crusty bread, a big cheese board, a dessert course of rich chocolate cake.

Olivier sits next to me at the table and my leg touches his. He draws me into the conversation, and it feels easier to take part. Around the table the chat goes from holidays (Tenerife, Budapest, Iceland, Palm Springs) to how someone's son was promoted, to how someone else had campaigned for new recycling bins in their apartment building. This last one prompts a long discussion where everyone brags about the good deeds they've done – volunteering, fundraising, recycling, zero waste – as though it's all a competition. I'm not sure who wins, but it leads into a more interesting (for me) conversation about the value and role of art in the current world. Claudette asks whether the others agree that all art should be challenging and have a purpose.

'Art does not have to be political,' Olivier says.

'*Mais si!*' someone responds loudly. 'Whether we know it or not, all art is political.'

Olivier's father fills everyone's glass, leaning across the table and talking as he pours. 'It may be. But I am not interested in idealism at the expense of aesthetic. When a work is powerful it can speak to history and politics, to love and hate and grief. But it must be first and foremost a work of art.'

'Don't you agree, Sofie, that art can exist to be beautiful and beautiful alone?' Olivier asks.

I do. I do agree with this.

Their French becomes fast and complex and it flies above my head.

'Can you understand?' Claudette asks at one point.

I nod and smile and let the conversation go on. I understand for the most part what people are saying, not that my mind is one hundred per cent following along. Under the table, Olivier softly runs circles on my palm with his thumb.

No-one looks at me and knows. They are busy with their opinions and their stories.

I feel different. I feel elated! Ecstatic!

No-one can tell I have just had one of the most transformative moments of my entire life. I am transformed. I love this night. I love all the food. But, more than that,

I love the feeling, the memory, the lingering sensation, of the kiss.

We end up leaving the party around 1.30 in the morning. Léon accepts repeated congratulations on his show, and Claudette retains her chic manner, in spite of the small red wine stain on her cream-coloured skirt, and she gives audible *bisous* to the entire party – *merci au revoir merci au revoir merci au revoir merci au revoir merci au revoir* – goodbyes that take forever, as custom would have it.

Olivier and I go unnoticed, mostly. I take my coat off the coat rack and look at him to try and work out what might be going on between us.

Merci, au revoir.

I am in uncharted territory and I need him to bring along a map.

He stands so close to me, and I breathe in his warm and spicy *parfum*, and he slowly kisses one cheek, and then the other. Not really kissing, but our skin softly skimming.

He takes out his phone and together we enter my phone number into it.

Merci, au revoir.

I hardly sleep when we get home. I lie in bed and feel as though I am floating on a wide, calm sea.

And Olivier has my coordinates.

19

How was the art show?

– Overnight chats with Crow (unopened)

I want to call Crow and tell her everything, but also, I want to keep it to myself and I also want to shout it to the world.

I have such a crush on him!

He has a crush on me!

I am sweet sixteen and I have been kissed!

It is a slow morning in the Durant household the day after the *vernissage*.

Bedroom doors stay closed even while I tiptoe around making breakfast *tartines* with butter and jam, and a giant cup of sweet tea. My feet feel like they hardly touch the floor I am flying so much.

I touch my lips to see if they feel different, still not quite believing the kiss.

I am boundless energy; I am hopped up. I need to get out of the house and I know where I want to go.

The Parc de Belleville is the biggest green patch between the Parc de Buttes Chaument and the Père Lachaise Cemetery, and Claudette had told me the view is worth the climb up the hill. Until now I've been drawn into the centre of Paris, pulled there by the must-sees, the iconic. I now feel ready to explore my own patch a little more.

And I have to get my body moving. I am ready to leap out of my skin. So I pull on my beanie and fly out the door.

My pace is fast, as fast as my beating heart, and I am very aware of my body in a way that is entirely new. It's like my limbs are learning how to move in the right way again, which makes sense when you think about how the kiss has probably scrambled all the neurons in my brain.

Belleville literally means beautiful town. This *quartier* is in the 20th arrondissement. The last one in the snail that makes up Paris's nautilus swirl, which begins at the centre in the posh 1st arrondissement. Belleville technically spreads across into neighbouring arrondissements too.

In 1871 there was bloody fighting along these streets. The Paris Commune wasn't the famous revolution with Marie Antoinette and the cake, but a socialist, working class, radical government. They had grand demands for the separation of church and state, and for ending child labour, but it lasted just two months and ended in a massacre at the Père Lachaise Cemetery just a short walk away.

I don't think Belleville is beautiful. Not the kind of beautiful you think of when you think of Paris. I imagine a lot of tourists never come here at all.

So maybe Belleville doesn't really feel like my idea of Paris, but it actually feels more like home now than all the cliché Parisian sites I'd longed for. There is a relaxed feeling to my adopted suburb, a comforting and familiar 'rough around the edges' vibe. It's the neighbourhood of graffiti and of loud open-air markets, and groups of people hanging out, chatting all day.

At the top of the park is a brutal-looking observatory. White and blocky stone, like something out of a depressing Russian movie. Classic Belleville. I aim for the top of the park.

I walk beneath the arches that cover the walkways, where the leaves that have turned bright yellow over winter poke in from the sides and cast a golden hue. There are some parts of the garden in the Parc de Belleville that are fenced off and locked with padlocks. There's a sign on one of the gates with an abstract picture of a reclining person and the words: *Pelouses au repose hivernal du 15/10 au 15/04.*

Shhhh. The grass is sleeping.

A month or two before I came away, I was helping Mum hang the washing out on the clothesline when she began a cringeworthy conversation.

'Would you like to see the doctor before you go away?' she asked.

'Why? Do I need a vaccination?' I was surprised because I thought I'd looked up all the requirements.

'No, no. I thought you might want to talk to them about contraception, you know. Just in case.'

I was glad to have a sheet hanging between us. I let my face press into the cool, damp cloth, but I could still see her outlined in shadow.

'No, I don't think so,' I said.

She had obviously been practising for this one. 'It's a very normal thing. An important thing. Being safe, you know.'

'I haven't even kissed anyone before!' It felt embarrassing to confess, but somehow less embarrassing than your mum thinking you were having *sex*!

'Well, you never know what will happen. I know you're smart, but don't be afraid or embarrassed to ask her for help. Claudette, I mean. Or the host sister.'

'Delphine,' I remind her. 'And I won't.'

At the time, this conversation felt so irrelevant to me. But now, it feels like something I could possibly start to think about. I'm not saying I plan on sleeping with him though! We've only just kissed!

Up up up go the steps to the observatory, and my thighs burn.

When I get to the top a sensation floods through me, like a rushing through my veins. I let out a big, happy breath and think about how it felt to kiss and be kissed.

The view is even better than I had imagined. I lean against the concrete lookout (not so ugly up close) to take in the entire city. Over the tops of wintry trees, to the Tour Montparnasse, to the Butte Montmartre ... from my vantage point, the whole city is mine.

And in my post-kiss glow, it is a paradise.

Paris is beautiful!
I am beautiful!
Everything is beautiful!
Even my suburb!
Crow! I type. *You'll never guess what happened.*

20

The following morning I wake up to a text from Mum that sends me crashing back down to earth.

There's a big bushfire tearing through the Bunyip State Park.

Is it bad? I write.

Couple of houses lost so far, she writes back. *And it's getting close to the house. Bit worried.*

Pop's not there now, on account of being in an old folks' home. But I can picture the house in my mind, and worry burns in my stomach.

When I was smaller, I think I was six, we almost lost the house. Black Saturday, they called it, and it took the entire country by surprise. There's a photo of me out the front with Pop – pre-dementia – standing on a patch of green grass right at the edge of the garden, and everything beyond the house is burned black. Trees reach up, leafless, into an ominous sky. I can remember how dirty my feet got that day, and drawing charcoal patterns on the kitchen linoleum until Dad shouted at me to stop and carried me to the bath.

Every summer after Black Saturday, I would get stressed

out thinking of bushfires, and I would pack my precious things up in case we had to evacuate. I even did this at home in the city, which was dumb. But thinking about it now, I feel really sad for little me.

These worries used to consume me when I was smaller. But then, I discovered drawing and art, and I found that when I drew, the worries went away.

So I stopped packing my bag of precious things, even though I still felt the twinge of worry each summer.

For a few hours, I scroll through bushfire hashtags online and scour news sites from home. There's some footage of helicopters flying above burning trees.

When my phone rings – Mum – my stomach lurches with fear.

'It went, Sofie,' she says, and her voice is tired. 'We lost the house.'

'Okay.' My voice is very small, and it's all I can say.

'I'm so sorry.'

'Why are you sorry?' My voice cracks, but no tears come. 'It's not your fault.'

'I'm still sorry. And I love you.'

'I love you too.'

After we hang up, I can't help going down a news spiral. There have been bushfires before, there have been floods and cyclones, but they're getting worse every year and no-one is quite sure what should be done about it. There are people who still claim that climate change isn't real.

The government has said over and over again that it's essential to invest in coal, that it's important for the

Australian economy. They say we're doing a good job at reducing carbon emissions. They give tax breaks to the rich mining magnates.

It's all lies, Crow's said in the past. They're even selling our water out from under us. If we don't cut emissions now, we're fucked.

For the first time in my life I am genuinely afraid that I won't have a future. Will I die by flood or fire or famine?

When can I get on a manned mission to Mars? Though as Crow would remind me, more money is poured into the barest possibility of Mars than trying to ensure the world we have doesn't end.

The world has been on the brink of ending so many times, and terrible things happen every day. I know this. I feel bad sometimes for thinking about kissing and boys when, in some other countries, people even younger than me are being blown up by roadside bombs. When the Amazon burns, and the Great Barrier Reef's coral becomes bleached and Bezos's Amazon workers are too worried to take toilet breaks without losing part of their pay cheque just so we can get anything we want delivered right to our doors.

And even though I know terrible things happen, I suddenly feel so terrified, as though my blood has turned to dirty lead in my veins. How is it possible that most of the time this knowledge just slips out from my head? I know all these things to be true, but it is very, very easy for me to forget them. Am I just as culpable as those who perpetuate this devastation?

~

Texts from Crow have come through while I was talking to Mum.

You heard about the bushfires here? They're just going to get worse if we keep dragging our feet on climate change.

Mum called me. Grandad's house just burned down.

Oh shit Sof. I'm sorry.

I feel far away today. I've been reading online obsessively. The fires are going to get worse?

Absolutely. And there'll be more in the future. I'm organising a march. We're walking out of school this Friday afternoon and going down to State Parliament together.

Even the teachers?

I dunno. I guess. Can you make us a poster?

I feel impotent. I can't even imagine what kind of a poster I'd make.

I can try.

I feel kind of robotic, and zinging with a low-level hum of anxiety. I wonder if that hum is actually there all the time. I think it is. But when I see something pretty or make something pleasing or hear a piece of music, it covers up the *pingingzing* and my heart swells instead of contracting.

I hate that being in France has made me so conscious of the thing that I do: use beauty to cover up reality. Because there shouldn't be anything wrong with beauty. It's beautiful, for goodness sake! Beautiful for goodness sake. For the sake of goodness. But is it covering up a multitude of sadnesses and truths? And is remaining ignorant about those truths damaging the world?

The world is ending. I know that. But what on earth can I do about it?

~

That night, during dinner with my host family and chats over tisane and chocolate afterwards, things still feel just as unbalanced and unexpected as my emotions. I don't have the words to explain what has happened back home, so I don't say anything.

No-one notices my silence because they are cranky about the *grève* – all the train drivers in Paris are going on strike, so the metro will be closed. It's in response to the explosion – they want better conditions, better pay.

'*Métro, boulot, dodo, rien n'a changé,*' says Claudette.

Delphine has been sitting on the sofa, a John Green book in front of her face. '*Oh là là, maman.* Spoken like a true *soixante-huitard.* You really have drunk the Kool Aid, haven't you?'

'Cynical child.'

'You were five years old in 1968. You weren't part of it at all.'

'But my father was out there on the Boulevard Saint-Michel digging up *pavés.* He was part of Dany le Rouge's circle.'

'And *your* mother? Where was she? Stuck in the house with a child. Like all women throughout time.'

Claudette does that thing with her mouth I'm coming to love from the French. An expulsion of air through the lips, a little fart/raspberry noise. She dismisses Delphine's point with this sound. She lets Léon know with this sound that she doesn't give two hoots they're out of toilet paper and in fact he should buy some. With this sound Claudette delivers a point of view without a word. It's generally combined with a slow rise of the shoulders, before letting them drop down again: point made.

'What are you talking about?' I ask, my mind briefly distracted from what is happening at home. I know they're speaking another language, but it's like they're *speaking another language*.

'In the 1960s, France was a very conservative country,' Claudette says. 'But it was a turbulent time around the world. You know, with nuclear bombs, the Vietnam War. But at the beginning of 1968 – my father was an engineering student – there was a big student uprising to try to modernise the universities. Then it expanded to all of French culture. They wanted to change the world. The protests went on for months.'

'Australians, do they protest?' asks Léon.

Of course they would ask me this today. Of all days.

'We protest,' I say. 'They protest …' I'm sounding like a lesson in verb conjugation. 'There are protests. I was just speaking to my best friend at home. She is organising a group of students for a protest this week. She is angry that our government refuses to do anything about climate change.'

I tell them the story – of drought and long summers and unstoppable bushfires. I try to explain about how our futures might be gone, but I don't know how to phrase it in any language. Before I know it, there are tears running down my face. 'And I know it's just a house, but—'

'*Oh là là*,' breathes Claudette. 'But that's such sad news, Sofie.'

'I'm okay,' I say, looking at their concerned faces. 'Really. I'm just sad.' I don't think I've shown this much emotion around the Durants before. I feel terribly far away from my family. I feel wobbly about the future I imagined. 'I'm just having trouble finding meaning today,' I say.

Delphine looks me in the eyes, and something about the look we share makes me feel better.

Claudette makes a round of tisane to calm our nerves. Léon shows us the new miniature sculpture he's been working on. Or he tries to. Delphine is back behind her book, *Tortues à l'infini* (I've read it in English: *Turtles all the Way Down*), and I'm reading about May '68, scrolling all the way down to the bottom of Wikipedia.

I feel exhausted when I lie down in bed, like I might cry again. Trying to think about Olivier and recalling our kiss feels weird and far away. I am older than I was this morning. I am different. I have cracked open.

I had to put my emotions into words today. I realise now maybe I've never had to do this. Before, when I felt sad or overwhelmed, I could slam a few doors or escape down the creek and know that come evening time I could sit on the couch with my mum or my dad and they'd let me cuddle into them, and ask me no questions.

The world is cracking open.

The world is ending.

Maybe one thing I can do is make some posters for Crow.

They protest. You protest. We protest.

I send: *OK. So what do you want these posters to say?*

I protest.

You protest.

We protest.

21

'Do you want to come for a run?' Delphine asks me, in French, the morning after the fire.

Her tone isn't soft, but it's kind. It reminds me of Hana when I'm being annoying but it doesn't bother her.

Claudette and Léon both look up from their coffee. Their clear surprise shows me that they haven't put Delphine up to this.

I go to my room and dig out the appropriate outfit. My mum would laugh if she could see me now. Voluntarily going for a run! I had contemplated leaving my running shoes and exercise clothes behind in Australia, but we hadn't been sure if there were sports components to school in France, so I thought I'd better be prepared (it turns out PE doesn't exist). This, two-and-a-half months into my exchange, is the first time I'm wearing exercise clothes. It feels wrong to be wearing them out in public in France though.

As we're going down in the lift, Delphine switches to English. 'I don't really have a running club,' she says dryly.

For a split second I'm embarrassed I've misunderstood

her. But no. She's in running clothes too. So what does she mean?

'You mean you don't have running club today?'

'Not ever.' She is smiling and searching my face for a reaction.

I want to laugh (from being uncomfortable) and I want to ask a million questions at once.

'Why would you make that up? It seems like such a weird lie.'

She laughs. 'Let me think. I like running. I run for exercise. And I run to get from here to there, but that's because I'm trying to avoid the metro. I hate being underground, in that metal box.'

'Where are you going then?' I ask. 'When they think you're at running training?'

We jog about a block and she doesn't say anything. I give her time. I side-step three dog poos (could have been one poo split into three) and wait for her to spill the beans.

'Well ...' she begins. 'You'll see.'

Delphine leads me, jogging, to a Belleville backstreet. I'm a bit puffed, and my face feels hot, but I'm completely intrigued. She unlatches a gate covered in overgrown plants, and I follow her through ... into a garden. I can't say what I was expecting, but it wasn't this.

It's just an empty city block about six metres wide, but I can't see how far back it goes. It's like a tunnel of green. Trees, creepers, and more green.

I step forward and before me are raised garden beds – one, two, three – framed in wood and heaped with straw. I can see pumpkins and a wheelbarrow. There are people here – I can see two people digging in the ground. There's a trestle table half set up to my left, its top leaning against the legs. As I turn to Delphine, in absolute delighted surprise, I feel her move. There's an older man coming out of a garden shed, holding an enormous soup pot.

'Let me help you,' says Delphine, and she goes to the trestle.

I help her lift the wooden tabletop onto its legs. The man grunts *merci* and hoists the pot onto the table. They greet each other warmly and give *bises*.

'Jean-Michel, let me present Sofie. Sofie, Jean-Michel. He's the president of this community garden.'

That's when I learn about *les jardins partagés*. As well as growing vegetables, fruit and flowers, they have a beehive and a weekly soup kitchen for refugees and homeless people and anyone else who needs it.

'That's what's happening today,' Delphine explains. 'A couple of days a week I come here and help to organise food and care packages to hand out to people in the community who need it most.'

Incredible! I feel my reality shifting once again and am surprised to find that this time I don't hate the feeling. Perhaps I am becoming accustomed to being out of my comfort zone.

'Why have you brought me here?' I ask. 'Not that I'm ungrateful. I'm very grateful.'

She smiles, and it's the most genuine smile I've seen from her. Some wall has come down. 'No real reason. I just thought you might like it.'

'Why don't you want your parents to know about this?' I ask. 'Wouldn't they be happy?'

She is quiet for a moment. I have sometimes felt uncomfortable in Delphine's silences since I first arrived in France, but I realise now that she is just taking her time to consider what she is going to say.

'I think I just want something for myself. I don't want them to be telling their friends I'm some kind of saint because I volunteer. My actions aren't currency for them to barter goodwill and feel smug about.'

We serve lunch to children and some adults, who all appear in the garden. My heart feels full, but it's also breaking in fifteen ways.

'The children are sleeping in tents?' I ask.

'Yeah,' says Delphine. 'Many of them arrived in France with no family. They're alone or here with siblings or maybe a family friend and have been camping in a park nearby. But they'll be moving on this week. The government is going to hide them somewhere.'

They're clearing the Paris streets of refugees. We have been learning about it at school, as part of a persuasive writing activity. The refugees are being sent to various areas around the country where the French government says there will be more infrastructure available. It sounds fair, kind of, but when you consider the realities it's hard to get on board with some faceless government body taking people who've fled persecution and danger and sacrificed so much and displacing them again, especially if they don't want to go.

Back home I live in a bubble. I haven't seen the realities of refugee and migrant life so close to my own. I knew it existed, but I tried not to think about it. Distractions come easily when you live in pursuit of beauty.

In Paris there are camps running along the side of the canals. I saw it on the news. The refugees set up tents on top of wooden packing pallets to keep the cold at bay. I don't even like camping on summer-hard soil when we go to Echuca on the school holidays.

'I've heard some migrants have drowned in the canal since the camps were set up,' I say.

Delphine looks grave. 'Yes. I can't help thinking that we've learned nothing in this country. In the 1960s, there was a massacre of French Arabs in Paris – mostly Algerian Muslims – after a protest against a curfew order. There's no agreed number of victims, but they pulled bodies out of the Seine – all murdered by the bullets, boots and nightsticks of the French National Police.'

'That's horrible,' I say, my hand flying up to my face.

Delphine nods. 'Back then, someone graffitied across a bridge: *ICI ON NOIE LES ALGERIENS*. Here we drown Algerians.'

I remember a photo from a few years ago, of the little refugee boy in his red t-shirt, drowned on a Turkish beach. As I learn more about the past, I feel disbelief about our present. How can we let the lessons of the past go unlearned? Are we doomed to make the same mistakes on a loop?

~

As the line dwindles and the last of the food is scraped from the pot, Jean-Michel asks me, 'Are you part of Delphine's running group?' He glances at her and winks in a cheerful, friendly way.

I laugh and shake my head. 'Delphine runs everywhere, but me, I walk.'

I watch Delphine, who looks so at home here. I can't believe I ever thought she was prim and proper. Now that I've seen her in action with a shovel I can't un-see it.

'Tell me about your walks,' says Jean-Michel.

'The only way for me to get to know Paris is to wander about without a plan,' I say. 'There are so many surprises when you wander without purpose. And I don't have much money, so I look for activities that are free to do. Walking has been the most satisfying one.'

I get my phone out and show him the maps I've been making.

Jean-Michel looks as though he wants to pinch my cheek, as though he thinks I am *charmante*, perhaps. Then he says something I don't fully understand – somethingsomething *dérive* – and then, probably because I look confused, he says, 'You know, the Situationists.' Not wanting to look ignorant, I just nod *oui oui bien sûr.* He wishes me luck before he gives *les bises* (right, then left, *mwah mwah*) and he is off, loping down the path towards the park's gates.

In my pocket, I've had a couple of messages from Olivier. *Salut. What are you doing?*

I'm out with Delphine, I reply. *How is your weekend?*

He sends a gif back of a cat wearing sunglasses, and no

other reply. I hadn't expected romance to be so cryptic. I shoot back a laughing face and put my phone away.

'Let's walk home past the Canal Saint-Martin,' says Delphine, coming back from the garden shed.

The bare trees and the white sky (it's just all over clouds) make the whole city look misty or fuzzy. Delphine leads me on a detour away from the canal, and to a *boulangerie* called *Du Pain et des Idées*, which has a queue out the door.

We eat and walk and talk. Well, Delphine talks, and I am so interested to finally get to know her I just want her to keep talking.

'I know I should be trying to eat a vegan diet,' she says. 'If we don't, the world is simply going to run out of resources. But I know it's a really privileged choice to make. Can you imagine those kids from today saying, *No thanks, I can't eat this because I only eat vegan organic*?'

I never expected Delphine's brain to turn in such ways. From outward appearances she is calm, poised, cool as a cucumber (cucumbers would make up a portion of a vegan diet, wouldn't they?). But when you get to know her better, you see she's wired, private, always thinking, always watching.

We walk back to the apartment, and I know I'm being quiet but I'm thinking about what Delphine and Jean-Michel have said. When we get home, I ask Delphine, 'Have you heard of the Situationists?'

'That sounds familiar,' she replies.

We look up the Situationists on her phone. While she scrolls down with her thumb, I watch her face all focused and serious (I wonder if I've ever looked that serious).

Olivier and Delphine would make such a handsome couple. Why does my mind go there? I feel jealous even thinking about it. I know she thinks he is just a rich kid. But he cares so much about art and people, and he is so interested in life – I just don't feel like she should write him off like that.

This is where my brain wanders while Delphine researches twentieth-century philosophy. I am a tiny bit ashamed of myself.

'So,' she says, looking up from her phone, but hovering her pointer finger over the screen like marking her spot on a page. 'It looks like the Situationists were social radicals from the sixties. Mostly avant-garde artists. They believed that capitalism and capitalist greed were destroying everyday life – *franchement*, I agree – and they came up with ways to subvert it. Through art and political pamphlets. It says that they were inspired by the Surrealist and Dada artistic movements. Ah, but of course. This is May '68 – I've seen these posters.'

Léon calls out something from the kitchen in fast French that I don't fully catch. I must have looked oblivious because Delphine calls back, 'Speak slower, papa.'

He comes into the room. 'Who was inspired by Dada and Surrealism?' he says, speaking slower but still in French.

'The Situationists,' I say, giving it my best pronunciation. *Les situationnists.*

Léon lays a hand across his cheek thoughtfully. 'I remember the Situationists. This philosophy was an enormous influence on the Atelier Populaire during '68.' He points to Delphine's phone. 'All these posters came out of the Atelier. The students occupied l'École des

Beaux-Arts after the government closed the universities during the strike.'

I imagine an occupation of our art room, all us students in a furious explosion of creativity and desire for change. It's a very good daydream seed, which I sow away for later.

Léon perches on the arm of the couch. 'And Guy Debord. He said TV, the media, the government, capitalism – all these things have made humans victims of "the Spectacle". A cycle of wanting and consuming not because of need or even desire, but in order to *look* as though you were successful.'

'This feels familiar,' says Delphine, and she puts on a chirpy voice and makes a face: 'Hashtag Instalife!'

'I feel like from its name, "the Spectacle" should be a good thing?' I say. It sounds so positive.

'So, how do they propose we break out of the Spectacle?' asks Delphine. The way she says it, the tone of her voice, her tight, wound-up posture like she's an animal ready to leap away at the whisper of a predator – make it sound like she is taking up a challenge.

22

I wear my most confident outfit in order to trick my brain into feeling the correct feeling.

Will I meet you at the atelier? I text to Olivier.

Oui, d'ac is his entire reply. Yes, okay. So short and sweet. I'd hoped for more enthusiasm.

It is almost a cliché of a set-up when we arrive for the life drawing class. The easels are arranged in a circle around a chair and a low, padded ottoman. Véronique is talking to a woman in a silky robe by the corner. You can tell they know each other by the easiness between them; they both look relaxed and are speaking in low tones.

'*Bonjour*,' I say to Fatima and give *bises*. '*Bonjour. Bonjour. Bonjour. Bonjour. Bonjour. Bonjour. Bonjour.*' (You have to say hello to everyone here otherwise you belong on the top step of rudeness.)

I do not feel relaxed. And it gets worse when Olivier arrives. I haven't seen him since The Kiss. My lips tingle with the memory of being on his lips. He has a delicate cream-coloured scarf knotted around his neck, looking like he has just stepped out of a Romantic painting. He just wears his jeans so well. My heart races.

He smiles and comes over to me and, somehow, he is able to be natural and calm. We give *les bises* and I worry my legs will give way beneath me. But I'm steadied by the way his hand lingers on the small of my back. I interpret this as his acknowledgement things have changed between us.

'Have you ever done a life drawing class?' I ask him, attempting to be natural and calm too.

'But of course,' he replies, in a way that makes me feel like I am weird for not having taken one before.

I go to explain that we just hadn't got to it yet at school back home, but Amandine calls Olivier over and then he is gone. I am left alone to set my station up: pencils, charcoal stick, drink bottle by my feet. I already need to wee from nerves.

I feel young and stupid and inexperienced. I hate that I am comparing nudity to sex. I know you can have one without the other. My brain KNOWS nudity is natural and nothing to be ashamed of. But the prospect of drawing someone naked makes me think of ME being naked. I haven't been naked in front of anybody since I was a little kid taking baths with my sister. And that was an *entirely* different situation.

I'd always felt like a prude during PE at school when we'd get changed – I'd always put my shorts on underneath my dress and do the complicated dance of pulling my bathers on underneath my t-shirt.

The model laughs, throwing her head back a little, making her long brown hair bounce. I feel very nervous about being in a room with my classmates and all of us staring at a naked woman for two hours. Especially now that I have been kissed. That I have kissed someone. And he is here. I feel so tense I want to cry.

'Hello, class,' says Véronique. 'Take your places.'

Over the next couple of hours I draw carefully, observing each part of the model's body in detail and with attention. I am relieved to realise that it doesn't feel pervy. I don't feel like I am judging her or laying a (fe)male gaze on her.

I am observing and re-creating her body in terms of its shape, its beauty, in a way: the aesthetic beauty of a curve here and a shadow there. I'm not analysing her body in terms of its sexual beauty.

Very quickly I feel embarrassed I was ever nervous or afraid of this.

I wonder what I'd look like if someone sketched me naked, even though I'm trying not to let my mind think what it is thinking. I refuse to let my mind drift towards a certain person in the room (well, almost refuse), let alone my gaze.

It is only later that day, after the class, when I am at home and looking at my sketches, that I take in her body. By then she is no longer the person I'd been observing in the classroom, not the human we'd been introduced to, who we thanked as she put her robe on once the two hours were up.

She's now become a series of sketches. I think in some ways I'd mentally put *myself* in the drawings. I always thought I was weird for having one boob bigger than the other, but now I wonder if everything is, in fact, normal. Everything is, in fact, beautiful.

I feel alive, I feel uncomfortable, I feel like I understand what desire is for the first time.

It is a coming home to my own body.

23

Maybe it's because of the life drawing class. Or maybe it's because I used six muscles I never knew I had while helping Delphine dig a new patch at the community garden. Maybe it's part of adapting to a new city. Whatever it is, I feel more comfortable in my body than ever, more aware of its potential.

Paris starts to feel familiar too; it feels friendly in a way it hasn't before now. When I arrive back at the house, the smell of coffee, laundry detergent, and even the musty elevator, envelops me and welcomes me home. The lift still clangs, and the hallways are dingy, but I like the way each apartment has its own style of decoration – sometimes a little wooden sign or an interesting welcome mat. There are prams and scooters by some of the doors and my mind goes spinning thinking about all the people who live inside.

My bedroom feels like it belongs to me, not like a borrowed Ikea room – there are clean clothes someone has folded and put on the chair for me; my pink blowsy scarf from the op shop back home across my bed; my pile of paper offcuts from Véronique ready for new drawings on the desk.

Olivier said to meet him at the Place des Vosges. Not far from the Rive Droite, in the Marais district. It is the oldest public square in Paris – possibly even Europe.

The Place des Vosges is a beautiful park – a square surrounded by terrace houses with red-brick patterns on their façades.

'They're all matching,' I comment.

'Most of Paris matches this way,' Olivier says casually (as if I hadn't noticed this about the city already! It's just that I continue to be impressed by it!). 'It's beautiful, don't you think?'

'Oh, it is,' I agree. I look up at a lamppost and enjoy the way it curls around so pleasingly – its lamplight dangling off the post like a fancy earring.

'When it is no longer winter, the trees are very green around the park,' he says.

'You can see the green starting to come through a bit,' I say. I turn a circle on the spot, to take in the whole square – park, road, matching rows of houses on all four sides. 'I wonder if any of the people who live here sometimes forget which house is theirs?'

'Well, Victor Hugo lived up there,' says Olivier, pointing.

I follow his gesture with my eyes. I know I should know who Victor Hugo is. But to be honest, I don't know what *anything* is when I'm looking at Olivier. His smile, his lips, his very being, bamboozles me.

'But can you be sure it was that one?' I ask, after a

moment's awkward pause. I grin, Cheshire Cat style, so he knows I'm making a joke.

He laughs a little (he is not much of a laugher) and lowers his arm, putting it around my shoulders as we walk on. I love the feeling of his arm around me, the way I fit in so snug. Is that how you know someone is right for you? When you fit together like puzzle pieces?

'Victor Hugo wrote *Les Mis*,' I say, remembering. '*Les Misérables*. I know it. Well, I've seen the movie.'

Olivier has an amused look on his face. Probably laughing at my pronunciation. Fortunately, I have decided not to get worried about that anymore. *Les mizzerables? Les miseraaaables?*

There are wooden benches all around the park and we sit on one, and I gaze around at the wanderers, the tourists, the older people having an afternoon outing in the crisp sunshine. It feels like spring might truly be coming to stay. I like the crunch of gravel from people walking and the sound of the fountain.

'Have you started working on your pieces for the exhibition?' Olivier asks, taking out his notebook.

'Sort of,' I say. It feels too early to tell. It feels too early to know if my scraps of ideas (my Panic Maps, my doodles of life and walking in Paris) will come out well enough to use. Over the past few weeks my personal brand of little art has started to seem … too little. Too disconnected from this big world I'm realising I'm part of. What does it mean when I see a tiny beautiful thing? Just because something is nice to look at, does that mean it's worthy of the looking? How can it become a piece of artwork that's meaningful enough and interesting enough?

Olivier doesn't press for more information, but he makes some sketches – a forest scene, of gloomy shadows and tall, somewhat overbearing trees. The detail he creates from out of nowhere is astonishing. I envy his talent.

While he sketches, I prowl about and snap photos of the *jardin*.

I notice that Olivier has put his notebook down and has his phone out, pointed at me. I take a photo of him taking a photo of me. Or at least I try to photograph him, but he covers his face with his hand (a classic Crow move, I actually feel quite nostalgic at the sight of it) and says, '*Arrête, arrête.*' Stop, stop.

Then he pulls me onto his lap. (His lap!) *Oh, my giddy heart.*

As though they have a mind of their own, my hands move to stroke the nape of his neck, and I run my fingers through his hair, all soft and curly. He leans into my touch like a cat nuzzling. I dip my head down and kiss his lips.

We sink into the kiss and for a moment I'm above my own body, floating above the Place des Vosges, looking down at a hopeful artist-in-training wearing an op-shop corduroy pinafore and a floral blouse, kissing an exquisitely beautiful French boy with curls like Louis Garrel. This couldn't be more perfect than if I had painted the scene myself.

I have always wondered when you decide to break off a kiss. I still don't know what the rule is, but it seems as though when you're kissing someone and you really like them and you realise they actually like you too, then whenever you stop kissing is just a pause before the next kiss.

'What are you doing now?' he asks. 'Can you come and eat?'

'Yes, I think so,' I reply. Inside I am both *What is eating?* and still floating, and also *Heck yes!* and trying not to drop my phone. 'Where will we go?' I start to feel precarious on his lap, self-conscious. It feels intimate in a way I'm not sure about yet.

He kisses me again. 'It's a surprise. Just you and me.'

'I remember you saying you have never had *escargots*,' Olivier says, as we sit down at a table near the window.

I try to take everything in. The marble-topped table, the bottle of fizzy water – plain *eau gazeuse* – the waiters in white shirts and black pants swooshing around like they have the dance moves memorised.

'So tell me more about your project for the exhibition,' he says.

'I've been thinking about trying to make a piece or a series of pieces about my trip here, and all the places I've been in Paris during my exchange. I'm not sure how I want it to look yet though.'

Olivier laughs when I make mistakes, but he pulls me back into French when I switch to English.

Before I came to Paris, Hana said as a joke that having a French lover would be the best way to learn the language. 'My baby is too young for a lover,' Mum had scolded her. 'Don't put ideas in her head.'

I don't feel too young now. I have travelled across the world, and here I am, sitting opposite a boy (almost a man) on a date in a French café, after dark, about to eat *escargots*. I did have to text my host family to let them know I wouldn't be home for dinner, but they'd just replied, 'No problem (*pas de problème*) – until later.'

He talks for a surprisingly long time about the new paintbrushes he wants to buy (I've committed most of the vocabulary for art supplies to memory by now: *un pinceau*), and I sip my fizzy water and feel amused but also somehow impressed at his dedication to paintbrushes.

'We walked past the Museum of European Photography on the way here,' he says.

'I didn't notice,' I confess.

'There was an exhibition of JR's work that I saw there last year. It was very interesting. We should go to the next exhibition there,' says Olivier. 'I would love to take you.'

A photography exhibition with Olivier! 'I would like that.'

'Have you heard of JR? He is a street artist. Makes large-scale photographic installations.'

'Yeah, I have,' I say, and I thank Crow for dragging me along to weird documentaries at the Cinema Nova. 'Did you see the film he made with Agnès Varda?'

'Of course,' he said. We smile at each other. Isn't it wonderful to have things in common?

The waiter brings our food over – an earthenware terracotta dish sizzlingly hot, with a strong garlic aroma steaming from it.

I look down at my plate, not entirely sure how to approach the meal. I take the opportunity to watch as Olivier starts eating, using his little fork to pop the *escargot* out of its shell. I'm reminded of the oysters.

'So many little forks in French cuisine,' I say.

'*Ceci n'est pas une fourchette*,' replies Olivier, pretending to puff on his fork like it's Magritte's pipe.

The joke and the moment are surreal. I can't believe this is my first real date. I don't feel like I can tell him that.

'I can't believe I'm about to eat a snail,' I say instead, smiling. 'What is my life?' I add, in English.

To be honest, while the garlic makes me think *delicious!*, the snails are chewy and rubbery and just a step too weird on my tongue.

'Remind me, when do you go home to Australia?'

My heart sinks. I am going to have to go home to Australia! Of course I knew this. But now I realise that whatever it is we're starting here will have to end.

'At the end of May,' I reply. I want to say: *I don't want to go.* But I don't want to scare him. I feel strung out, like I am tuned too tight.

'There's still a long time until May.'

24

Crow

I'm impressed you ate the snails.

Sofie

I had to – it would have been
so rude otherwise.

And at least you BOTH had
garlic breath.

The garlic kisses were pretty good.

Gran's making garlic bread tonight …
Mum's in town.

You ok with that???

Yeah. It'll be fine. Maybe I'll hang
the garlic round my neck.

XXXX

– Overnight chats with Crow

In *Sciences Économiques et Sociales* (my Economics and Social Science class) we are studying how we create and measure wealth. We are also supposed to be learning how we become 'social actors'. I am still a little unclear on the meaning. It is reassuring when I finally just sit back in class and let the words and conversations wash over me.

'Did you understand?' asks the teacher from time to time.

'*Un peu*,' I'd said at first. A little. Then, when my confidence built, I'd say, '*La moitié* (half),' even when I'm not sure I do understand exactly half, but it is near enough.

I take notes like maps. Poverty to wealth. Like the American Dream. We studied that in history class back home too. This idea that all Americans could be whatever they wanted to be, that it was their god-given right to expand west across the map, taking no note of who had come before and whose paths they were treading upon, whose stories they were rewriting.

Someday this information will be useful to me.

'You like beautiful things, don't you?' asks Delphine one day, out of the blue.

'I do,' I say, wondering where this is going.

'If you aren't doing anything this weekend, we should go to the *marché aux puces*.'

'*Oui, d'accord*,' I say, agreeing.

The *marché aux puces*. I know what this is; it's the flea markets. I've read about *les puces*. (I've been pronouncing it like the colour puce, like 'pewce'. Turns out it's more like 'poo-se'.)

'Cool. I'll play tourist with you,' she says. 'I have to go quickly to the gardens early in the morning, but how about we find ourselves tomorrow at the metro around ten?'

To be clear – she is just saying 'let's meet at the metro', but 'we'll find ourselves there' is the literal translation of the French. It might seem silly that it took me so long to understand, and maybe I shouldn't focus on the literal, but that's how I've been getting by. Half understanding.

Maybe one day I'll be fluent, and when I'm fluent I'll translate differently in my head. But for now it's a process. Understand the French words. Translate them back to English. Interrogate the words for the correct meaning.

For example, when Delphine said angrily to Léon the other day that the way the government has ignored the *gilets jaunes*' demands and at the same time encouraged the right-wing racists makes her shit, she didn't mean it literally. *Ça me fait chier* just means she's really angry about it. She's not actually pooping with rage.

We haven't even gone down the stairs into the metro station when we run into Olivier. I immediately burst into flames, and I hope no-one notices. *Mwah mwah.*

I want to ask him to come with us, but because going to *les puces* wasn't my idea, and I know the French stand on ceremony, I keep my mouth shut, careful not to offend.

'See you soon,' he says, coming close to *faire les bises* goodbye. I feel his hand on my waist and hope I don't liquefy under his touch.

'Is there actually something going on between you and Olivier?' asks Delphine, as I watch him walk away.

I'm not sure how to explain what we are. We haven't had the conversation.

Olivier and I have messaged and he's sent crooning texts telling me he hopes to see me soon and asking how my sketches are coming along.

I'm not brave enough to say I think he might be my boyfriend. So I just say, 'Yeah, we are good friends. He helps me with my art.'

I worry that my face and the heat I am radiating will give me away.

Delphine doesn't say anything, but I feel as though she thinks he is a bit of a wanker.

She just doesn't know him the way I do.

But, then again, I am smitten like a kitten.

On the way we see a series of posters that have been put up in the metro. They are blocky illustrations or prints or something. I've seen one of them a few times now – a simple silhouette of a factory, with a fist rising from the smoke stack printed in red, in black, in an inky blue. The text changes from poster to poster. Sometimes it's *Macron démission!* Macron resign! Sometimes: *La lutte continue.*

'The fight continues,' translates Delphine.

There's something so simple and powerful about the posters. They're handmade, or designed to look like it, and so the art and the artist don't seem far away from each other. But they are arresting and smart. I try to take photos when the train stops at the stations.

'This is a really common kind of poster,' says Delphine. 'Like we were looking at the other day. It was popular during May '68. This is what Jean-Michel was talking about at the garden.'

I'm startled to realise I know what she means. Suddenly, other connections synapse and whizz in my brain. May 1968. Paris. Protests. Guy Debord. The Situationists. *The Society of the Spectacle*. I am still trying to make sense of it all, but what I do know is that the posters are so interesting visually, as well as in their context.

I think about what Delphine said. How do we break out of the Spectacle?

I try to not think about Olivier as we catch the metro to Porte de Clignancourt, changing at Barbès–Rochechouart. Out of the metro and under an overpass, then we are beyond the *périphérique*. We're not in Kansas anymore, Toto.

Paris's main arrondissements all fit inside this almost oval-shaped part of the city bordered by the *périphérique*, a freeway of sorts. Outside this are the suburbs, which in French are called *banlieues*. I hadn't crossed into the suburbs since first arriving.

Saint-Ouen, the district where the markets are, is rough. I feel nervous, which I haven't often felt in Paris. Okay, a little in Belleville at the start.

But then, after a few blocks of trash-and-treasure market stalls, we arrive at the undercover goldmine of antiques and vintage gems.

Time stops having any meaning while I am at the flea markets. I keep forgetting Delphine is there as we rummage carefully through each stall selling trinkets and crafts, clothes and furniture. In a saucer full of button badges I find one that says: *Soyez réalistes, demandez l'impossible.*

Be realistic, demand the impossible. It's in black type on a red background, and I buy it immediately for Crow.

Here is a list of the things I see, covet and photograph:

1. Deep sea diving suit.
2. Vintage boots and dresses to die for (where I get told off for taking photographs).
3. Boxes of vinyl records.
4. Teacups and saucers.
5. Burnished silverware (and dirty silverware).

'You take a lot of photos,' Delphine observes as I scoot away from a dress stall, the owner wagging her finger at me.

I slide my phone into my pocket. 'Do I? Too many photos?'

She shrugs.

'It's because I try to put up at least one photo a day on Instagram,' I explain.

She laughs. 'I think Guy Debord would judge you and your attachment to the Spectacle.'

25

This is the night. *The* night. The best of my life, and one I will remember forever.

Claudette and Léon have gone to Bordeaux for the weekend. They're going to be away for two nights, and while I don't set out to immediately break all the rules (my host family's rules, Toby's rules, my parents' rules), that's just how it plays out.

I have, however, planned how this night might go, since I read about the concept of the *dérive*. It is a way of moving without great intention through an urban environment, letting the footpaths, buildings and surprise encounters direct your route.

Delphine shrugs when I tell her I'm going out. 'Just make sure you come home,' she says. She doesn't want to come with us, so it's just me, Olivier, Léa, Amandine and Victor.

It all starts at 59 Rivoli, which was once an artists' squat (before that it was surely some rich person's house or a bank or something), and you'd be forgiven for thinking it's still an artists' squat. As you walk in from the street, it's like someone's painted a welcome message and then forty-five other people have had a go on top of it – bright colours and shapes graffitied on. The effect is haphazard and inviting – as though everyone is welcome here and anything goes.

We climb the staircase, which is painted just as bright and lurid as the entryway and which spirals up and up, and we visit the studios filled with artists. They're creating Modernist and Postmodernist and Anarchic art, and the walls are all covered in colour and pattern and slogans.

'Imagine having a space here to create and display your art,' says Olivier. 'I can see myself here.'

'Me too,' says Amandine, as she sits on a little stool in one of the studios and immediately looks at home.

'I don't know how I would feel having people walking through and seeing my unfinished pieces,' I say. 'I wonder if it would be like them seeing you half naked.' I blush as soon as I say *naked*, and don't look at Olivier for a good minute. Thankfully everyone moves on into the next space.

I like the concept of this place, but I also wonder about these artists whose sketches and ideas are automatically part of the show. Their drafts look just as curated as the finished products. Where are the real flops or aesthetically jarring mistakes? I think of how I sift through photos to find the best one to add to my feed. But what about the ones where my finger creeps into shot, or the selfie where I've failed to consider the angle properly? I think about Delphine and Guy Debord and the Spectacle. Maybe there's a place for keeping these in view. Maybe the naked and unfinished are more powerful, and shouldn't be deleted or kept to yourself.

There is a band playing in a big dark room, and that's also what we've come for. African beats thud right through me, rolling and building and pulling me into the dance. The band raps and the crowd sings and the beat beats on.

We dance. People throw their arms up and close their eyes, and I've never really been part of a scene like this before – I didn't even know I liked this kind of music. Léa wiggles around me and I feel so anarchic! Like the world is offering so many things to me, and I can invite in what I want and push back on others. I am wild and I am free.

Olivier comes close and he smells like oil paints and spicy cologne, and his hands feel good around my waist. Our bodies touch as we move with the music and the crowd, and I've never danced like this before with someone who likes me. I've never danced like this with *anyone*.

When it begins to get more crowded, the vibe starts to change and we decide to leave.

'*On se dégage d'ici!*' says Olivier. Let's blow this joint.

'Get ready, everyone, for our all-night *dérive*!' I say as we spill out onto the street.

I explain the concept of the *dérive*. 'We just walk,' I say, 'and let our feet take us where they want to go. We allow ourselves to make discoveries.'

'And then what happens?' asks Victor, whose cigarette glows red like a tiny homing beacon.

Guy Debord says you need to follow the contours of the city, but I'm not sure how to say contours in French. And anyway, if we can't find the contours – which we might not, as I don't know what they look like – I have a secret weapon.

In my pocket is a fistful of scraps of paper with little directives written upon them: turn right, turn left, take the second left, go straight ahead, spin around the next lamppost, take five steps to the right and take a photo, now take a selfie.

'The *dérive* will help us travel to places we might not already know and will open us up to surprising situations.' I think I've understood it right. 'Are you ready?' I ask, looking around at my friends and making my voice a bit mysterious. 'We are in this together. You can't *dérive* on your own.'

'We will be explorers of the night,' says Olivier, and he wraps his arms around me and lifts me off the ground – I haven't been lifted up since I was a kid. It's freeing and fun and frightening all at once. He laughs, probably because I am squealing (in a classy and romantic way, of course).

'Which direction shall I take you?' he asks.

We are just delighted to be alive and to be together. I feel light and like I am exactly where I am supposed to be.

Everyone knows Olivier and I are together, and it is the first time in my life that I'm part of a 'thing' – that I'm paired.

I catch his hand and pull him alongside me. '*On va par ici?*' I ask.

He wipes a smudge of pizza sauce from my lip and licks it off his thumb. His lips are beautiful, and I burn and spark when I think about how those lips have kissed mine.

Then he pulls me gently in the direction I'd indicated and waves to the others. '*Allons-y!* Let's go!'

We are so young. So free. *Liberté, egalité, jeunesse!*

~

We dance on the Alexandre III bridge, and the Eiffel Tower's light show delights me, even though the others make fun of me, and the whole experience is yet another reminder that what I am doing is amazing. I know my experience is special and privileged. It's as though I am in a dream or a movie and, appropriately, the city turns it on for me.

It is warm enough that I leave my coat unbuttoned and we wave at cars and shout to passers-by as we drift along the river.

We take videos, a constant stream of Insta stories. For a few hours we make films. We run alongside the houseboats on the edge of the Seine and get some superb footage when I accidentally disturb some ducks. Our conversations are inconsequential.

There's fog descending and it makes the lampposts cast yellow pools of light. Red lights from the cranes dot the horizon.

Olivier and I kiss on the deserted forecourt of Notre Dame cathedral. It is 2 am. Victor, Léa and Amandine have gone to find more food, but I'm not hungry and it seems like Olivier isn't either.

This is proper kissing, and it turns out I *am* hungry, in a way.

I want you, I think (but I don't say it. It feels terrifying and too soon). I don't think my body has ever felt like this before. Not even in my many, many dreams, not even the most vivid.

Even while it is happening, I'm thinking, *How do I know how to do this?* And I feel astonished by instinct and animal nature. At first, I think human nature, but actually humans are idiots and I swear it's the animal in us that leads this part.

Olivier holds my face as he kisses me, like they do in the movies.

Time stops, and there is even a moment when the ground under my feet disappears, the great cathedral is gone from my consciousness, and we are suspended alone, in a dream.

I am glad when Victor, Léa and Amandine come back – wielding crêpes and singing, inexplicably, *La Marseillaise* (the French national anthem, of all things!). It feels safe to have my feet planted back on the ground, to have gravity reinstated. I never expected love (or whatever this is) to be so destabilising.

'Did you know they keep bees on the roof of the Notre Dame?' says Victor.

'Bees? For honey?' I ask, staring up at the gargoyles, the flying buttresses, the delicate beautiful spire.

Victor nods and smiles. Bees and beehives have always seemed so functional and staid to me, but in a flash they take on a magical quality.

Our night is like Paris in a painting. We are drifting in the fog in an Impressionist urban landscape, and I have to pinch myself and shake myself, and it all feels delightfully unreal.

We buy croissants from an early-opening bakery on the Rue des Abbesses and stave off eating them until we have walked up the hill. I am starved. Our *nuit blanche* (our white night, our all-nighter) is making itself known, but we trudge up the hill anyway, pressing down on the tops of our thighs for momentum.

We walk up to the Butte de Montmartre and sit on the steps below that mighty Sacré Cœur to look out over the watery dawn of Paris.

We pass around the croissants and they're still warm inside the thick brown paper bag. Flaky crumbs fall onto the stone steps, which are so cold that I take my sketchbook out of my bag and slide it underneath my bum.

It is the most wonderful view. Perhaps even better than from the top of the Parc de Belleville because this one is being shared with friends, and with a buttery croissant and a warm arm around me. I give Olivier a little kiss just for no reason.

Amandine points out the Centre Pompidou – blue and red and yellow pipes that rise above the city. Victor extends his arm to indicate the Gare du Nord, an expanse of flat roof. Léa, indefatigable, performs an arabesque – her toe pointing perfectly straight out behind her and her arm raised in a way that points to the tippy top of the basilica.

'What I'm going to do,' I say, my head resting on Olivier's shoulder. 'I'm going to make a pencil and watercolour sketch with all these buildings waking up.' I wave my arm across the sky to demonstrate the buildings I mean.

'That would look pretty,' Olivier says.

'And it will be in blues and greys with white space and blurred lines.'

Olivier's fingers are entwined with mine, and he says, 'I can see it already. You've made a beautiful drawing.'

I'll call it *L'Aube. Dawn.*

All I need is some good quality paper.

Tourists have started to arrive. Olivier photographs the tourists. He then takes a photo of me and turns the camera around to take one of the two of us, snuffling his face into my neck and leaving light kisses that tickle and make me thrill.

Our *dérive* has taken us through back streets and has disoriented us appropriately. Though we ended up in the least secret place in the city, my mind does feel opened and reset and renewed.

I am happy, I am tired, I am surprised, I am elated.

26

I have signed up for a printmaking workshop at the École des Beaux-Arts one Monday afternoon in mid-April. Our art teacher, Véronique, is leading it and encouraged me to come along.

In French you say *gravure sur bois* for woodcut, or *gravure sur linoléum* if you're doing a linocut. When I told Olivier about it, he said he wanted to come too.

I take the metro over to the 6th arrondissement, where the classes are held. The 6th is the one in all the photos: Saint-Germain-des-Prés and the beautiful Boulevard Saint-Germain and the expansive, duck-filled Luxembourg Gardens.

Because I am a keen bean, I arrive in the 6th way too early. *I could have walked*, I think grumpily. I go into a newsagent and buy a copy of *Les Inrockuptibles*, a music and culture magazine, to pass the time. Fortunately there's a nice bench to sit on, and as I leaf through the pages, I learn some interesting slang. I'm impressed with myself for working out the words. It is like doing a puzzle.

There is an article about the new craze for protest signs

and posters. The posters are amazing. They feature the same imagery – the factory with the fist – as the ones Delphine and I looked at online and in the metro. These ones use fluorescent inks in greens and yellows and hot pinks, and shout: *Your house is on fire.* I can't tear my eyes away. I forward one, two, three to Crow. Maybe we could use this idea if she needs posters again sometime.

She sends back: *!!!!*

Her reaction is more affirming than Olivier's had been. When I'd first brought up the posters from 1968, he had laughed. 'Everyone loves these,' he'd said, scrolling through them on my phone. 'I do like the simplicity. But I don't know if my father would hang these in an exhibition.'

'No, probably not,' I'd agreed. But afterwards I wondered if I did agree. These are historical documents, they're creative expressions of the time, and they've become iconic imagery. What is it that excludes them from worth as art?

I watch the city pass by, and I sketch what I think the subterranean route might have been that the train took to get here. And onto this map I mark the things I saw on the metro that I would have missed if I had walked:

1. The fat baby of a begging Roma woman bobbing out of its sling.
2. A canoodling young couple.
3. A tiny old woman in a fur coat with a tiny dog on her lap.

The building, the École des Beaux-Arts, is itself a work of art – though I've thought that about every building in Paris.

Inside, we are a small class of about eight people, so we can get close as Véronique shows us Li Hua's work *Arise*, which is full of fear and movement. She talks about Matisse, John Banting, Picasso, Warhol – and even mentions the Atelier Populaire.

And then it is our turn. Choosing what to draw for the linocut is very stressful. Usually when I draw I can just flip to the next page if I'm not happy or rip a page out. But this time I have to decide on something I would be happy to print again and again. Oh! The pressure!

Olivier is more confident about choosing an image for his linocut. 'I thought I'd experiment with light and dark,' he says to Véronique, and shows her a version of the tree drawing he'd done, the one of the haunted forest with the commanding trunks stretching up to the sky.

I feel slightly happier when I learn we're just working on little squares. I tell myself that it's just a practice. Just a first go.

And so I start my first linocut. I figure a word is a simple place to begin, and I go with *Rêve*, French for dream. I carve it mirrored, to print the right-way-round.

I learn how to hold the lino up to the heater to make it easier to run the tool across it. I learn which tools work best for the kind of lines I want to make and how hard to press. I learn that the tools are sharp, and I subsequently have to learn the word for band-aid (*un pansement*).

Once we are finished, we roll the ink onto our lino squares and run the press slowly over them. Holding onto the press wheel makes me feel like a captain steering a ship.

I hold my breath as I peel the paper from the lino,

and can't stop a smile as the print comes away almost perfect. When I lay it out on a table and look over it, the imperfections (not enough ink rolled on, a little smudge, a bit of dirt trapped in the ink) actually give it extra life.

Olivier gently pinches my finger, the one with the band-aid. 'Nice.'

For my second go I am bolder. I take a bigger square and I cut the simple map I made of Paris. Bordered by the *périphérique*, I outline each arrondissement and I slice the whole city through horizontally with the Seine. It's an approximation of Paris, but Paris nonetheless.

'Are you happy with it?' asks Véronique, looking over my shoulder.

'I am. I have an idea for my exhibition project,' I say tentatively. 'And I think this class is helping me get closer to being able to see it.'

'Do you want to tell me more?' she asks.

I try to think where to start. 'Maybe soon,' I say, and we share a knowing, happy smile.

27

I don't even notice, but the workshop runs a little late.

We step out into the evening around 7.30 and wander along the Rue des Beaux-Arts.

'Remember I want to take you to Shakespeare and Company,' I say to Olivier. He slings his arm over my shoulder.

'A lot of sirens,' says Véronique, tilting her head to listen.

I hear them too, but there are always a lot of sirens in Paris. More than back home. Their tone here is more commanding too, at some kind of pitch that causes them to ring out: *bee-barp bee-barp.*

'Until tomorrow, you two,' says Véronique, and she strides off towards the Boulevard Saint-Germain.

We walk the other way, heading towards Shakespeare. At first, I'm distracted by having Olivier's arm around me, and by imagining a stranger looking at us and what they might be thinking. Can they tell that I'm not French? Does the beanie knitted by my grandpa give me away? Do we suit as a couple? The tall thin artist with a cigarette tucked behind his ear, and the short, big-hipped girl whose hair pokes scrappily from under her shabby hat?

I soon realise there is a strange movement of people around us. The sirens shriek louder than ever. A feeling of unease grows in me and shifts like seasickness with the movement of my steps.

'Wait, look at that.' Olivier points, and his arm drops from my shoulder.

I follow his arm to the sky, where ominous smoke billows above our heads.

Remember, the world is ending.

There are more and more people on the street. I feel crowded. Everyone is breathless; our pace increases and I have to run to keep up with Olivier's long-legged stride.

As we come out on the Place Saint-Michel, we see it.

'*Oh mon dieu*,' say voices around me. So many people with their hands over their mouths.

The Notre Dame burns orange. Flames leap and smoke billows.

It's like a movie. Like a nightmare.

We hurry along, pushing through the crowd to get closer. Through the alleyways I visited on my first day, with the kebab shops and crêpes and felafel. The shops that sell souvenirs for tourists. We come out by the Shakespeare and Company bookshop, and we've got front row seats to history in the making.

I watch Olivier's face, transfixed by this scene, as we stand there, and I am reminded of the night he walked me home. When it felt like the world was ending.

'Do you think anyone was inside?' I ask, though even as I say it, I'm not sure why he'd know.

The initial flurries turn into a quiet reverence, people comforting one another, just watching it burn. The image of Jean-Pierre Houël's *Storming of the Bastille* flashes in my mind – that black smoke, those tiny people.

Then my grandfather's house flashes in my mind. As it was, when I was a kid, and how it is now. Rubble. Charred.

Maybe things can't last forever.

Beautiful things can disappear.

Accidents happen.

What about the beehives? I wonder. *Those poor bees.*

Some people begin singing.

I don't know the song, but they all raise their voices, and it's magical to be among it.

Terrible things happen, but sometimes they're beautiful. Or stunning, or life-changing.

And we stand there.

Singing the cathedral down.

28

Crow

What did it smell like?

Sofie

Do you know, it didn't smell like anything?

That smoke was thick though.

I know. And such a weird colour.

Scary.

Very.

– Overnight chats with Crow

Everyone talks about the Notre Dame fire for days.

Friends (and not-friends, but people who like to be involved in d.r.a.m.a.s) from home all message me, and I feel this really weird sense of responsibility and relevance, as I send photos and tell them how actually I was *right there*.

In the heat of the moment I had posted a photo, taken

from where we stood that evening on the Rue Saint-Jacques. It is the most-liked and most-shared post I've ever had, which is a bit disappointing. I've worked hard to build an audience for my drawing, and find followers and validation for the tiny beautifuls I capture. It feels a bit gross to be benefiting from this.

I'm so glad the cathedral didn't burn to the ground. I don't know how that would have felt. The structure's still standing, with only the roof gone. It is so strange and perversely wonderful to think I was there to watch it happen.

But I also get it and find myself a bit obsessed. I draw a sketch of the cathedral and loop lines around and around it, to mark all the times I go to check in on what's happening with salvage and repair. There are always many people checking in. I do it in spite of myself. I know that it's just a building and that terrible things happen all the time, that in the grand scheme of terrible things it is not the most terrible; the internet is ablaze with sympathies and criticisms alike.

At least the bees are safe!

I read the newspaper headlines and there are more and more things I understand as I find the French language easier. *Crise!* they say. Crisis.

Since the fire, so many billionaires have donated to a rebuilding fund and millions of euros are piling in. I think it's amazing, and staggering. I find it hard to imagine that amount of money.

Crow sends me an image she found online. It's a poster. *Sorry for the inconvenience. We are trying to change the world.*

The poor are getting poorer and the rich are getting richer, and people are speaking up. They're making plans. They're saying enough is enough! There's no life on a dead planet.

It's not our fault, say the richies. It's not our fault we're good at our jobs. We're hard workers. If the poor worked harder, they would have more money.

Mum got a promotion at work once, and I was excited imagining the presents she might buy me with her new money, only to be disappointed by something called a 'higher tax bracket' that meant, somehow, she had less money in her pay cheque each month.

And where are the millions to rebuild Grandpa's house? To turn climate change around? End poverty?

I want to believe I can change the world, writes Crow. *But I think we need to start by eating the rich.*

Delphine invites me to come to a meeting on Friday night, at her friend's house out in the suburbs. She and her friends are preparing for a march – a *manifestation*, she called it. *Manif* for short.

'We want them to declare a climate emergency and we want to show the government that we don't agree with their proposed economic changes.' When Delphine speaks, I feel moved, and I feel like I can change things too.

I send a text message to Olivier: *I'm going to a political meeting. Do you want to come with Delphine and me?*

No response.

So we tell Claudette and Léon there's an evening session for running club, and off we go.

At the meeting I don't understand a lot of the conversation and for once I don't think it's a language thing, but an ignorance thing. But I put a look on my face that hopefully shows I'm an ally. And that I should be there.

I still next to a girl called Manon, who has hair that curls and drops all the way to her waist.

They talk and they're so informed about subjects from climate change, to American politics, to the ramifications of Brexit, to gender violence. I wonder how do you decide what cause is worth fighting for the most?

'Can you believe these billionaires have already donated all that money to repair the Notre Dame roof?'

'I agree it's outrageous, but is it so bad?' says someone else. 'It's a cultural icon. Shouldn't we preserve it?'

'It's disgusting,' says Manon. 'Nine hundred million euros after just two days. These people could change the world if they wanted.'

'But they don't,' I add. 'Do you know, in a strange way, I feel lucky to have been there when it was on fire. I don't think I've been part of history like that before.'

Delphine leans in. 'But you have.'

I am confused.

'We all are right now! We are witnesses to the sixth mass extinction. We're on the frontline of history. And those in power are doing nothing. It's up to us to make them sit up and pay attention.'

I have never thought about climate change this way. We've always known about it. Learned about it at school. How can it be that children know there's an emergency, but our governments knowingly sit by and just let it happen? I almost don't believe it.

But looking around at this group – they're mobilising. They're taking this seriously.

I could make more posters. I've got the skills. I've got the words to say, 'I would like to make some posters, if that would help you.'

The group looks at me, their faces friendly, encouraging.

I smile and say, '*Donnez-moi vos slogans!*'

They give me their words and I sketch them out.

While we paint and draw and paste, the world hums around me. I am part of it, but I am also somewhere else. I feel like this might be what people who meditate are trying to achieve. I love having something to put all my focus into. It's how I always feel when I make art, but there is something more to it tonight.

We talk about metaphors and rhetoric and sometimes I don't understand exactly why something is clever or funny, but they take the time to explain some strange intricacy of language or some years-old reference from TV. I feel as though I learn more about the French language in four hours than I've done in class for two months.

'Did you know …' I say, channelling Crow, my voice cutting through the hubbub. 'Did you know that half the coral in the Great Barrier Reef is completely dead? It boiled to death.'

'Well, that makes me depressed,' says Manon. 'I've never even seen the Great Barrier Reef.'

'Me neither,' I add. 'Don't forget the pollution from sunscreen and the effect mining has on the coral reefs. And speaking of boiling, did you know that if you boil a frog in water really slowly, it never realises the water is getting hot and it just keeps swimming around until it dies?'

'We are the frog!' shouts Delphine. I can't believe I ever thought she was a demure piano-playing French girl. I'm starting to wonder if she's secretly Joan of Arc.

Between us, we bring my sketches and their intentions to life. I help them fix bits of wood to the cardboard signs with thick gaffer tape. They call the tape *ruban adhésif.* I'm learning so many handywoman words!

I feel proud once we are done. I am elated and exhausted in equal measures when it is time to leave.

'*Merci, Sofie,*' says Manon, kissing one of my cheeks and then the other. '*À la prochaine.*'

I can't stop thinking about all that dead, bleached, boiled-to-death coral. Shake it off, shake it off. There is absolutely nothing I can do about the coral. Though Delphine thinks there is. Maybe, maybe she is right.

I feel guilty about my parents, who seem to get by without worrying all that much. I feel guilty about my easy life. About being able to come here.

I call Hana to say all this and more. To pour my guilt out.

'I am so privileged. How am I supposed to be part of this? How can I be outraged, when I'm part of the problem?'

'You are privileged,' she says. 'We both are.'

'I want to be part of the movement.'

'You can be. Just do it. You have just as much to offer as the next guy.'

'I don't know that I do.'

'Sof, we might be privileged, but we're also smart enough to know it. And we may have had it easy in terms of enough food and safe housing our whole lives, but we also have perspective. We can see those who have too much, and Mum and Dad have tried to keep our eyes open to the world. There's no ivory tower here. I work every day with people who have completely lost perspective – if they ever had any to begin with – on what's right and what's good in the world. It's disgusting.'

'How can you bear to take their money then?'

She's silent for a moment. 'Because I'm going to take their money, take it right out of their greedy hands. And I'm going to do something great with it. I know Dad doesn't believe me, and he thinks I've sold out. But just wait.'

My sister, an activist. Maybe I shouldn't have been surprised.

29

I thought I'd try selling some prints and cards on the street. My cash stash is dwindling.

I set up at the top of the Parc de Belleville and I send out some Insta stories to let my friends (in both countries) know where I am. Delphine lent me a picnic blanket that belongs to her parents and I've made a little sign with prices and information. I've tried to mimic the French style of writing with its loopy cursive letters. I line up my pieces on the blanket.

I've sketched people, buildings, even particular trees (because there aren't so many) around the *quartier*, and have copied them out multiple times on some beautiful card. I thought I'd charge two euro each, because they're quite small.

I won't say my little art stall is buzzing with business.

'How was your meeting?' asks Olivier, appearing from around a nearby corner.

'It was really interesting,' I reply. 'You should have come along. We made signs to carry at the protest.'

I sell two illustrations to some cute-as-heck backpackers.

The ones they choose are of a pair of lovers in beanies: one of the couple kissing on the forecourt of the Notre Dame and the second showing the pair photographing each other in a park. I want the tourist couple to think maybe the drawing could be of them (that's why they bought them, of course). But surely Olivier knows I've drawn us. I've memorialised us in illustration and set ourselves into the world. I think it's romantic.

'You are a hawker, like the guys selling cheap Eiffel Tower keyrings,' laughs Olivier.

I try not to be offended.

'It's not like I'm asking for much money,' I say. 'Not like the shops that charge double or triple the price of art and trinkets and sell them in hip stores.'

'Instead you're selling out your own work for cash.'

'But what about all those paintings you've talked about in your parents' house? Your family paid money for those.'

More shrugging. More *bof*. 'It's not the same. That's an investment. I'm just saying you're talented. I worry you're devaluing yourself.'

When he says it like that, I kind of understand. But also, sitting on my high horse valuing myself won't help me buy paper, pencils, croissants. So I just shrug. 'Thank you for saying I'm talented.'

Olivier holds up the new bookmarks I've made. 'Where did you get this paper?' he asks, rubbing it between his thumb and finger.

'They're offcuts from school. That's why I've done these pieces so small, to get the most use out of them.' I feel happy with my thriftiness.

'But how did you get it?'

'I just asked Véronique if I could have it. She was putting it in the recycling.' I open my homemade folio and pull out some more pieces, bigger this time. 'She let me take some of these slightly damaged sheets too, for my exhibition piece. They'll be useful, once I decide what I'm doing.'

I recently learned the expression *faire du lèche-vitrines*, which translates to 'window shopping'. But actually, the direct translation is 'window licking'. I immediately had to sketch a series of self-portraits of me slobbery licking (like a dog) the windows of iconic Paris shops: Chanel, Maxim's, Ladurée.

I show these to Olivier, and he shuffles through them with a strange expression on his face. 'Funny,' he says, in a *that's really not very funny* voice, and tosses them back onto the rug.

He's also not interested in more serious conversation. 'Did you know that by 2030 the richest one per cent will own two-thirds of global wealth?' I ask him, and by now I'm – on the inside – begging him to have an opinion. To react!

'*Et alors?*' So what?

'Don't you find that staggering?' I ask.

He shrugs.

I don't say anything more, but inside I am sighing because I don't know how to make him feel the way I do, and I don't understand where he stands. I can't explain, in English or French, why those numbers frighten me so much or exactly how they will impact us all, but I just feel it. Feel the fear.

'It is interesting,' he says, finally, sitting down next to me and slipping his hand into mine. 'And you are such a good person to be worrying about these things. But let's talk about art, instead.'

When I've had enough selling for the day (a grand total of twenty-four euros – I'm happy with this!) we go to Olivier's house. He wants to show me the art that was an investment but not a capitalist sell-out. It is the first time I've been there since Léon's *vernissage*, and this time it feels *significant*. This time I am very aware of my body and less aware of the beautiful apartment.

I feel hungry but it isn't a mealtime, so Olivier doesn't offer me anything to eat. The French are so strange like that. I miss snacking.

He leads me down a hallway by the hand, waving at some paintings with his other hand. We pass the dining room I'd sat in that time, with its long table and antique chairs. Now, instead of plates of *bœuf bourguignon* and glasses of wine, there are piles of newspapers at one end, and a pair of abandoned (but very chic) men's eyeglasses.

He leads me to his bedroom and for a while we look at his books, arranged in his shelves that go up and up, filled with new and old books and knick-knacks and whatnots. We talk about the objects, about nothing in particular. Situational chitchat. I couldn't even tell you because he leans against his desk, which is big and made of dark polished wood and has complicated legs, and the sight is too much.

I think about sketching him there, against the backdrop

of a Parisian window. His navy shirt is buttoned all the way to his throat. I can see rooftops and the kind of light that's limping to dusk, and I feel very romantic.

I say so, and I press against him, fitting myself between his legs. 'Is this okay?'

He nods. 'Is this okay?' he asks, as he slips his hand under my shirt.

'Yes,' I say. (And it is.)

We lie down on the bed.

'Does it feel good?' he asks.

'Yes,' I say. (And it does.)

But I'm not ready for it to go much further. I want to, but also, I don't. '*Je ne suis pas prête*,' I say, kissing his temple before pulling back to look at him, and have him look at me. 'Does that bother you?'

'It's not a problem,' he says, kissing my temple in return. 'My little kangaroo.'

The last of the day's sunshine comes in the window, and we lie there together as my dreams come true.

30

'Could you walk to Versailles?' I ask Toby, as we get on the RER C train at l'Étoile. RER is a suburban rail, and this particular one will rocket us from the centre of town out to the famous palace – is it the most famous palace in France? Is it a *château* or a *palais*? *C'est quoi la différence?*

Toby rocks with the movement of the train as it accelerates away. 'You mean from here?' he says, holding on to the pole.

I nod.

'Yeah, you technically could. It would take you half a day though. But today we'll walk from the train station up to the château, if you're worried about getting your steps in.' Toby laughs.

I don't laugh back, even though I know he is making a joke. Toby is a crowd-pleaser. I don't *not* like him, but I find his jovial nature a bit irritating. I had hoped to surround myself with serious artistic people. He's not exactly what I had in mind when I pictured my guide to France.

I've missed out on some of these group activities – getting Léon to send apologies, citing a busy school day or a minor illness. Between art class, Olivier, the garden, and selling my wares up on the Belleville hill, there's been so many other things to do! But when the exchange organisation arranged an outing for us all to the Château de Versailles, I thought I would go. Students came from all over the country and we were spending the weekend together.

While city and suburbs flash past, I hear about rural life in France. It's fascinating! One girl – Hollie, the red-headed art fan I met at orientation – is living in a three-hundred-year-old farmhouse. Australian Rupa lives with a host family that own a horse-riding academy, and she gets to go riding all the time.

Another guy, the puffer-jacketed American called Dan, stands up, raises his hand and says, 'Well, get this. There is this guy in my village, a plumber or builder or something, I forget. But I'll never forget his name because it's on the side of his work van. You ready? Jean-Claude Fromage!'

The group whoops with laugher.

Dan's grinning his face off. 'Can you get more clichéd?' he asks.

Later, I'll tell people that the Château de Versailles is grand, stately, historic, with an opulence that is overwhelming and all-consuming. I can't say what I actually think at the time because my mind boggles when we walk over the cobblestones up to the castle entrance. There are busloads of tourists, but I remove them from view as I take in the centuries of history.

'Kings and queens walked along here,' I say, unbelievingly,

knowing my tone is irritating with wonder. I can practically hear the clop of horses' hooves on the stone.

'And plenty of servants,' Dan shoots back.

'And plenty of servants,' I agree.

The guide ushers us through the tour route, through vast rooms with shiny floors and rich tapestry-and-paint walls. The hall of mirrors is more than I had ever hoped, glittering in the light. Astonishing to think of all the work it takes to keep this place perfect for us.

I particularly love walking through the bedrooms with tiny high beds, and I lean against the ropes to get as close as possible so I can observe the detail. I picture myself in a giant powder-blue gown with rosettes and embroidery, swishing across the stone floors in wood-and-silk slippers. I was extraordinarily beautiful and graceful in the past.

'I love living history museums,' I say to Rupa. 'But it's a version of the past, not a reality, isn't it? We're getting an idea of how it would have been. And a very sanitised version,' I say, surprising myself with my insight.

'Literally,' she adds. 'I mean, there weren't flushing toilets. Or proper bathrooms. I love thinking of how bad people would have smelled back in the day.'

'Gross,' says Amelia, who is from California and whose favourite part of her exchange so far has been learning to make macarons. As yet I haven't learned to cook anything, so I make sure to put 'learn a few impressive recipes' on my to-do list.

I agree with Amelia about the grossness, but also, like Rupa, find it fascinating.

I think about all the staff who made things work

centuries ago. The distance they had to travel just to bring water or *un petit café* from the kitchens seems unreal.

The grounds of Versailles are muddy and lush under the pale blue sky. A couple of birds titter around the fountain and the canal, and I imagine taking a bath in the cold water would not be pleasurable.

Marie Antoinette's hamlet is a highlight for me – so charming! – but Dan and Rupa snort in unison when Toby explains how the Austrian queen had ordered this village built so she could swan about with the swans and collect eggs from the chickens, watch the servants mill the grain and the bakers bake bread. A place for her to pretend she was one of the people.

The air is different here. The sky is brighter. The smells are different too – fresher. I lie on a patch of slightly damp grass and look up. The trees stretch into the blue, shaking their new leaves cheerily.

I draw a miniature village in the bottom corner of a page in my sketchbook – here is the church, here is the steeple – and I leave plenty of room above it for sky. I add a speck for a bird and some faint almost imperceptible pencil lines for sky dimension – cloud, light, jet streams.

I can see why someone would build themselves a village.

Dan and I sit together on the train back, with Hollie and Rupa opposite. I am exhausted from all the socialising and the sightseeing. He is comfortable to be with, and the girls are easy to talk to.

'Did you know,' starts Rupa, leaning in, 'I was reading yesterday about how there was a women's walk from Paris to Versailles in 1789. Seven thousand women marched from the city to the château—'

'During the revolution?' I interrupt.

'That's right,' she continues. 'They were demanding the monarchy release the bread they'd been hoarding.'

'Let them eat cake!' Hollie cries, in a very good Marie Antoinette impression.

'The mob beheaded two of the queen's bodyguards or foot soldiers or whatever. They demanded she come out and explain herself. It was a huge moment in the revolution.'

Dan, Hollie and I are all looking at Rupa, captivated.

'I dunno,' she shrugs. 'I just keep thinking about it.'

Sometimes it feels as though there are things holding me back from truly understanding moments like these. Like a veil across comprehension. Sometimes I can't stop myself thinking about other things: Olivier's fingers in mine; a rude comment on my most recent Instagram post; my ideas for my exhibition piece.

Now, I'm not distracted though. I look around at these new friends, and I feel like I'm present in the world like never before. 'People *en masse* have more power than we realise.'

31

All of a sudden, it gets warm. The temperature is in double digits on the regular, and we have a run of beautiful spring days. I dream of daffodils.

Me and Crow decide to take a day to do a *dérive* together. We've arranged it all – I had this idea that we could walk and map the same routes in Melbourne and in Paris simultaneously. We'd take it in turns to make the choices – turn left, turn right – so we'd be exploring together in different cities.

If it works the way I've hoped then I will use it for my exhibition piece.

I have saved up my phone data so we can FaceTime the whole *dérive*, and Crow has done the same. I have become very smart at finding free Wi-Fi over the past week. I also haven't looked at Instagram nearly as much.

'Will we just walk until we get tired?' Crow asks. She's painted a row of silver dots just below her brow, following its curve. It looks amazing against her new electric blue hair.

'Sounds good to me.'

Delphine wants to join us too. 'If that doesn't derange you,' she adds.

Crow laughs, an awkward I-probably-shouldn't-laugh-at-this laugh.

'Bother,' I say, nonchalantly. 'If that doesn't *bother* us.'

We begin at our front doors – Delphine and me outside the gate with its keypad for the long code (which I've long-memorised) and Crow slamming the door to her gran's flat hard so the deadlock catches and stays shut (there's a trick to it). Debord says we should just follow the natural – or, I guess, unnatural – lines of the urban environment. But like last time, I've got a secret pocket full of directions if needed.

As we drift, we discuss philosophy and poverty, and Crow and Delphine talk politics and how to find a voice. We talk about history. I tell them a little about Olivier.

Even though my heart leaps and my pupils dilate and my body still goes electric when I see him, I find myself wanting to see Olivier less and less. It is uncomfortable thinking. Something's been off between us since I went to his house. It's like we've run out of things to talk about.

He takes photos of me but only posts very vague things on his Instagram. Like, I know one photo is my eye, but no-one else can tell. His feed is elusive and abstract and impersonal. Like the way he's been acting in art class this past week.

'*L'amour, ça ne m'intéresse pas*,' Delphine says eventually. Love doesn't interest me. 'I love my parents, in the way you must love your parents. But I think they're flawed people.'

I realise Delphine has known her parents a lot longer than I have, but I do think she's being harsh. We're all flawed, really. However, I admire her confidence in her opinions. I'm less sure about where she sets the bar for loving people though.

Delphine is more interested in the cause. 'But I am not interested in romance. I am not even that interested in physical contact.'

'I feel exactly the same,' says Crow.

You learn new things about people all the time. I forgot, or maybe I haven't ever really considered, that not everyone has romantic or sexual feelings. This part of me is only just newly swirling as I'm learning what I like and what I want – but I think I always assumed this is how a person feels. I am grateful to be reminded that mine is not the only way.

'Your little slips are counterproductive to the *dérive*,' says Delphine, her voice cutting through my thoughts.

'What do you mean?' I ask, my mind torn away from Olivier and this tiny flash of something like insight. I'm glad to be distracted from it.

She gestures at my pieces of paper. 'We have to truly let our minds go. You can't construct a situation. We have to free ourselves from the Spectacle.'

As we walk, unguided and unprompted, we talk about veganism. ('I just love cheese,' I admit.) We talk about the future. 'If we even have a future,' Crow says grimly.

'Do you know what?' says Delphine. 'I think we will. I don't know what it's going to look like, but I know we have to make it ourselves – oh wait,' she says, stopping in the middle of the footpath next to a supermarket. 'Wait one second.' And she darts into the shop.

On my phone I can see Crow is in a Brunswick West street, just footpath and houses and gum trees around her. I can hear a dog barking somewhere. It's so familiar and now, suddenly, so far away.

'So how long does a *dérive* last?' she asks. 'It's going to get dark here soon and I'd better keep an eye out for Stabby Joe.'

'I miss you,' I say. It just comes out.

Her hood obscures her face as she looks down for a moment. When she looks back up, I see a hint of her smile. Then her face returns to her normal serious expression and she adjusts her headphones. 'I think I've talked to you more than I ever have before, since you've been away.' Her tone is mean, but I know she doesn't mean it. I am in love with how our friendship has grown.

Delphine is back, and she's pulling at my sleeve. 'I want to show you something.'

We go through the supermarket, and I try to film the shelves for Crow (she loves detail too) but Delphine's keeping a good pace and I imagine all Crow is seeing is a blur.

At the back of the shop there's a door ajar, and Delphine raises her hand ever so slightly in a secretive kind of wave as she pulls me through. I catch a glimpse of a supermarket worker guy, but then we're going up some metal stairs.

I gather we're not meant to be here. But Delphine runs up the steps with the confidence of someone who knows exactly where they're going, whether they're allowed to be there or not.

On the roof of this supermarket there are rows of planter

boxes filled with tomato vines taller than me, and plenty of other fruit and vegetables. 'Are they growing food to sell downstairs in the shop?' I ask in delighted surprise.

'They are,' says Delphine. 'It's a new craze here in Paris.'

'It's revolutionary!' I say with a tone of wonder I'm immediately embarrassed by.

Delphine laughs, but she's nodding. 'I hope it catches on. Can you imagine – this is how Paris would have been in the olden days.'

'I mean, it's still a supermarket,' says Crow, who is sitting close into the camera and taking this all in from a world away. 'It's still selling things to people for profit, and a lot will probably go to waste. But it's a start. It's fucking revolutionary.'

I make a plan to recut my simple Paris map, but this time on a large piece of linoleum – at least A2 size. I want to print in different coloured inks, but not black. Maybe pale blues and pinks. I might experiment with yellows.

I'm out of big paper though. I had asked Véronique if there were any more large bits of scrap I could use, and she'd told me unfortunately they were all gone. Down at the *papeterie*, the stationery shop, I couldn't justify the costs. So for now I'm using some cardboard I found in a big leaning stack on the street – freshly dumped, so it's dry and mostly undamaged (thank you, Belleville, for being a bit of a rubbish dump).

I mark our *dérive*, across two countries, on one map. The points are the conversations we had, the corners we turned, the spot where Crow trod on a snail – mostly we let Crow choose the route, and she decided in split seconds based on decisions she couldn't describe. All leading to the supermarket so we could watch the plants grow and then buy their fruit. I label the maps with landmarks from both Paris and Melbourne.

I consider landmarks. What exactly constitutes a landmark? A very tall building. Your house. Supermarkets. Parks. The corner of a street in a city where I first successfully eavesdrop on a conversation. A breeze on an elbow.

And now I know the world is ending, I see it. It's all around me. But, at the same time, how great can this world be! We walk around, our feet tripping over history at each step, over centuries of human happiness and misery, and stumbling into possible futures while we're at it.

Fucking revolutionary.

32

On Wednesdays I don't have classes in the afternoon, so I leave Maths with a literal skip of joy. I want to shout *oh là là!* But I have to rush because I have arranged to meet Olivier, back up the top of the Belleville hill to sell cards and prints and bookmarks.

Side note: this venture has improved my counting-in-French and currency skills considerably. I don't have to think much about the numbers when making change, and I know all the coins and notes by sight now instead of having to hold each one up to read them like a tourist.

Olivier lies on the picnic blanket with his head in my lap, scrolling through photos on his phone. I run my fingers lazily through his curls and occasionally dip down for a kiss.

'You're beautiful, you know?' says Olivier, putting his phone down for a moment.

It is so very strange how I've become *used* to him telling me I am beautiful. But I have become accustomed, in some way, to Olivier's crooning, mushy sweet nothings. Did I know? Did I know I was beautiful? What does it mean to be beautiful? Does it even matter?

In this moment, at the top of Paris, I should feel on top of the world. But I feel … unsettled.

We need an artist photograph for the exhibition catalogue.

'Hey, do you have those photos of me?' I ask.

'Which ones?'

'From the Place des Vosges? The day we had *les escargots*?'

I watch him stare into space for a moment, before saying, 'I deleted them, I think.' He goes back to his phone. 'Sorry.'

Am I wrong to feel offended? He's brought his folio, so I pick up some of his sketches to distract myself, to feel the paper between my fingers.

'Did you buy this paper?' I ask.

'I got it from Véronique,' he says casually. 'Like you did.'

Heat rushes to my face.

He sits up. 'Do you want to see what I've been working on for the exhibition?'

He shows me some photos on his phone and for a second I'm not sure what I'm looking at.

Maybe if someone else were to look at them, his artworks wouldn't remind them of anything at all. The one that stands out is a painting of a face, done in oils.

But it's my face.

His new work, his work for the exhibition, is inspired by maps. Specifically mapping a way to know a person and a place.

'I want them to be portraits of people, photorealistic portraits. And I will superimpose the lines of their palm onto their faces.' He traces a line across my palm, but I pull my hand away. His idea is horribly, suspiciously like my idea. 'It will represent the lives they have lived and the paths they have taken.'

Not only is he a paper stealer – when he could definitely afford to buy his own – but he's an ideas stealer too! It's even worse to know he's used my face in his picture. He's taken other people's faces, palms, bodies too.

I knew he drew me. I thought he was being romantic. And I liked the idea of being someone's muse. But if I'm his muse, why I am so annoyed that his painting of me looks really good?

I know he's chosen oils so he can show off his technical skills perfectly. The rich colours and brushstrokes. I look at his paintings a little bit longer and feel troubled. In my heart my maps, my demonstrations of a life lived, are starting to feel silly.

'Sofie? What do you think?'

'What do you want me to think?' I ask. I have no idea what to say. I want to shout, but it feels stupid. I look into his face, like if I look hard enough I'll understand how I'm feeling, why I'm feeling this way, and what I should do about it. 'These are just like my ideas.'

He shakes his head. 'Not at all. Our work is very different. This has been inspired by Agnès Varda.'

But I know he's lying. He can't look me in the eye.

'It's still a bit strange. People will think we've copied each other.'

He lets out one of those Frenchy puffs. *Bof.*

'Well, then, why don't you do those slogans you're always talking about?' he asks. 'Or some still life. Your pears are looking much better these days.'

I've done many sketches of slogans and loved doing them. It's exciting to create pieces quickly that are bold and loose. But they're copies and interpretations of other people's work. 'Why would I want to do that?'

He shrugs, Frenchly. *Bof.*

'Anyway, that's not the point. Why would you steal my concept and then try to push me to return to still life – a style you know I'm trying to branch out from?'

'Oh, calm down,' he says.

I may have been a bit angry before, but now the blood rushing through me is made of fire. I pack my things into my backpack, neat bundles of the creations of my heart. It comes out in a rush: 'I don't want this anymore.'

'What don't you want?' he asks.

'You and me.'

He is quiet for a moment and as I watch his beautiful hair blow in the light breeze and his perfect skin glint under the limpid sunlight of early spring, I want to take it back.

'Why?'

'I don't know.' The truth is, I do have some ideas why. My frustration is partly because I don't have the words to explain. Not words he would understand. And I can't work out if I want him to fight for me, to win me back, to show me that we matter, that this beautiful little thing we've been creating together matters.

'Is this about my pieces?' he asks.

'Yes!' I shout. I want him to click, and to apologise, and to consider what he's done.

But he merely goes back to his folio and says lightly, '*Comme tu veux.*' As you wish.

I do not wish it.

I am incensed.

I get up. I get up and I walk away. It takes everything I have to not look back. Perhaps I would turn into a pillar of salt. If I turn around, I know I will shatter. Dissolve. Go running to him.

Later, at home, I hate that I can still feel his hair in my fingers.

The weight of his head as it laid in my lap.

I call Hana and cry and cry. 'Art is dead. My heart is dead.'

33

Crow

What a fake!

Sofie

Crow I'm so disappointed! I can't bear it!

I'm so glad you broke up with him.

I'm not.

Really??????

Ok yes, fine. I'm glad it was my decision. But it sucks.

Yep.

– Overnight chats with Crow

I stop hearing from Olivier. I guess I should've expected it, but still. I miss the messages coming through and seeing his name pop up on the screen. I miss his messages with the *bis* at the bottom. Shorthand for kiss. Something like xx.

I miss the real-life *bisous* as well.

I try to enjoy my heartbreak. That was Crow's advice.

Don't all great artists find their muse in broken hearts and depression? she texts.

I don't think we should be glorifying depression! I write back, a bit shocked. The shock shakes me out of my blues a little, which is annoyingly helpful, and I realise I have been enjoying wallowing more than a little.

You know what I mean.

I see him in class and in the atelier of course. He says *bonjour, ça va, salut*, as though not much at all has been lost, and I echo the same salutations back to him from an empty and shrunken place. I feel so sad, even though it had been my choice, my action.

Map of Olivier – this is the map I made the day I ended it with him. That night I took a fresh copy of my map of Paris and I marked all the places we had been together.

But this sparked a furious making of art. Maps. *Détournements* and poems. But mostly maps!

1. Places I saw a dog poop.
2. The kinds of dogs I've seen and where I've seen them.
3. Every croissant I ate and where I bought it from (I made this one into an art piece where I glued croissant crumbs onto a piece of paper and labelled them).
4. Places I saw a street cleaner with one of those green brooms.
5. Places where someone vaped *right into my face* (there were a lot of stops on this map).
6. A photo essay of every pharmacy I passed on my

way to school (seven of them, and nine on the alternate route back home on the same day – nine *different* ones).

7. Days I had a sore throat due to the pollution (this was just a list of dates, not my best work).

Between what's going on back home and what I am seeing here, not to mention everything that happens on the news, it's hardly surprising that I am blue. It really feels like the world is ending.

Remember, the world is ending.

I'm feeling every emotion that bit more sharply. It's as though I've been through some kind of portal from naivety to this uncomfortable new mature, experienced state.

We troop out of school on a Friday afternoon, Léa and me and Amandine, and they're talking about their weekends. Amandine is saying she is going shopping because she really wants a new dress for the exhibition, and I'm half listening, half worrying about my piece for the exhibition.

'That woman is staring you up and down,' says Léa, suspicion in her voice as she lights a cigarette.

'What woman?' I ask and follow her gaze. Follow it all the way to a very familiar face across the road.

For a second I feel the most intense confusion as well as a lurch, as though the world is spinning or tilting and I don't know who or where I am.

It is Hana.

How can it be Hana?

'*C'est ma sœur!*' I cry.

Later, Léa calls me reckless, because apparently I ran

right across the road without looking for cars. She calls it *l'appel du vide*. The call of the void.

I don't remember doing that; I just remember seeing Hana like seeing a very welcome ghost.

I throw my arms around her.

'Put your hat on, honey,' Hana says as she hugs me back. 'We're going for a walk.'

34

I want to show Hana all of my favourite things.

All of the weird and the wonderful. Like the Arts et Métiers metro stop on the 11 line, which is all chrome and metal and looks like a scene from a dystopian movie, or a really fancy submarine.

'Will you be here on Saturday?' I ask.

'No, I'm only here for two days,' Hana says, apologetically. 'I have to be in Berlin to meet some friends, and then I'm heading to Greece for two weeks. I'm going to volunteer with a group who helps women and child migrants in refugee camps outside of Athens.'

'What about your job?'

'Oh, I'm still slogging away there – I haven't escaped yet. But I've taken a few weeks of leave. I had to do something constructive.'

I always feel so proud of my sister. I picture her as a tree, with good strong roots that help her stand tall and straight and unstoppable. She's the tree that if a bushfire came through and turned her trunk black and burned off all her leaves would burst forth with new green foliage after the very first rain. Determined. Unbreakable.

'What's happening on Saturday?' she asks.

'There's a *manifestation* planned. Sorry, a protest—' I secretly thrill at accidentally using French instead of English, a genuine accident. 'Delphine and I, well, I'll go along with her friends – we're planning to protest for action on climate change. We want climate justice.'

'Tell me about it,' says Hana in a world-weary tone. Then, bumping me with her shoulder, she adds, 'I'm so glad you're finding your voice, Sof.'

We look at each other. The age gap between us feels like it's closing more and more quickly. Is this how it works? I'll leave my teen years behind (well, not for four years) and then Hana and I will reach some kind of sisterly equilibrium? Does she feel it too?

'I don't know if I've found my voice,' I say. 'But I feel like I've sat too quietly for too long. I'll shout extra loud for you.' I smile at her and link my arm with hers. 'Tell me more about Greece.'

She tells me about the organisation. It runs art and craft activities for children and women – making kites, puppets, jewellery – to give people something to do, as well as hope.

'I want to be a bit useful, at least. I'm going to work on some funding applications with the founder there.'

My mind races. 'I would love to do something like that.'

'Maybe you will. Maybe you're already preparing for it with your new worldly outlook?' Hana pinches my cheek like a proud grandma.

'Get off,' I say, laughing. But a seed has been sown. What kind of tree will I be?

~

Hana has read all about the best coffee in Paris and so we visit a whole bunch of places I haven't been before.

Her favourite is this Belleville café (I've never even seen it before!) not far from the canal. 'It looked *très classique* on the website,' she tells me. 'And they do music some nights. What a dream.'

When we get there, I see what she means, what with its blue canvas awning and the wicker chairs pushed tight together around little outdoor tables.

'We'll just have to imagine that scaffolding away,' Hana says, right as I'm thinking exactly the same thing. 'In our memories of our visit here, there'll be nothing blocking our view.'

She pays for my five-euro flat white (from a barista with an Aussie accent) while I reel at the cost. She tells me stories from home, surely exaggerating the madcap behaviour of our parents, and as she speaks, I wish she could stay longer.

But I figure we can fit in most of my favourite things. I show her all of my haunts. As we leave Du Pain et des Idées with many iconic blue bags of bread and pastries, Hana eyeballs me.

'What?' I say, feeling uncomfortable.

'Nothing.'

But it isn't nothing. I pull the top off a baguette and eat it. Hana continues to say nothing, but is still giving me side-eye.

'What?!'

'I just can't get over you speaking French.'

'Well, we're in France.' Secretly I am ecstatic that somehow I've become someone who actually speaks another language.

'I know. But you're so good! You were such a pro back there. I feel like I need to get to know this new Parisian-inspired sister.'

Is she thinking I've grown up during my time here? Do I *feel* more grown up after these four months?

'Shut up,' I say, not sure how to cope with her compliments or my own self-growth.

'You eat so much more than you used to,' Hana says. 'It's good! It's nice not to share a meal with a bird.' She takes a bite of her *escargot de pralines*, *pistache-chocolat* flavour. Stopping in the middle of the footpath, she closes her eyes and hums with delight.

'You're what we'd call a *gourmande*,' I explain.

'*Oh là là*,' teases Hana. 'What we'd call a *gourmande*.' I don't even mind the teasing; it's just so nice to have her here.

I even show her one haunt I hadn't wanted her to see, but it's accidental. By the Canal Saint-Martin, Olivier is sitting on a park bench in his black jeans, his hair all ruffled. My heart throbs in spite of itself.

'What's up?' asks Hana as she pulls me onto the footpath.

I've stopped walking in the middle of the street. *Très* uncool. 'Don't look, but that's him.'

'*Him*, him?'

'Don't look!'

Hana looks behind her, at her watch, scans the quay. I watch her trying to keep a smile off her face. 'Well, I don't blame you, sis. He looks like a right young Bob Dylan,' she reports. 'Charming, but pretentious as heck.'

'That old wrinkle?' I reply. 'He does not!'

'Does too, you poetic little cliché.' Her tone is condescending, but with a warm humour that reminds me of our mum.

'Anyway, I hate him.' I start walking off.

'Don't bother hating him, Sof.'

I glare at her.

'Or do!' She holds her hands up in mock surrender. 'Yes! What a dick.'

'Exactly. I hate him.'

If there were a voice-over to my life right now, it would probably say: *She doesn't hate him. She feels silly for having fallen for him. She feels betrayed on a visceral, artistic level.*

Though I wish it hadn't been Olivier, it is still somehow special that we ran into someone I know. On the street. By chance. In Paris. This city feels like home more than it ever has before, more than I ever thought it might.

Back at the apartment, there's something different as soon as we open the door. Music is coming from somewhere. It's a fast, disjointed tune – I don't know much about jazz or whatever this is, but even I can tell it's a song well-played.

With her door open, we can see Delphine playing the keyboard. Her back is to us, but she's playing with her entire body. The notes shouldn't work together, but they do.

'She's incredible,' says Hana, her voice low and full of wonder.

All I can do is nod and listen. We stand there until the song is finished, then I tug Hana's sleeve and pull her into the kitchen.

It's not long before Delphine comes out. I can see that she wants to ask how long we've been home, but I want to let her keep the song to herself. She's shared so much with me already; I ought to let her have this.

'I'm so glad you're here,' I say. 'Delphine, meet Hana – my sister.'

I almost feel guilty for a moment, like I've replaced my sister with another. But as soon as I see them together – Hana warmly leaning in to *faire les bises* with a confidence I wish she'd trained in me, and Delphine relaxing into a chair and pouring out three cups of tea – I know there's nothing to worry about.

With Léon working at his atelier and Claudette late with a *réunion* ('It means meeting,' I explain to Hana), it's me this time who takes the Tupperware from the fridge and puts together a meal for us all while my sister and my host sister talk. Travel, politics, food, work.

'But why do you work there if they are so immoral?' Delphine asks, and I wait for my sister to jump down her throat.

But Hana just shakes her head. 'The money makes me feel safe somehow. We didn't have that when I was young. But I have an escape plan. I just hope I'll be brave enough to put it into action.'

Delphine doesn't push her further.

I want to show Hana I support her, so I say, 'I think if we keep talking about what's important then you'll get out when you need to. We just have to remember not to get sucked into the Spectacle.'

'Honestly, where'd this part of you appear from, little

sister?' Hana smiles. 'Show me what you've been working on.'

And so I bring out my folio and show her my Lonely Homesick Maps, my Panic Maps, and my ideas for the exhibition.

'*Oh là*,' says Delphine and leans across to brush some dirt from a page. 'That's from the garden. Sorry.'

'I meant to say,' says Hana. 'Did Mum tell you the trees are starting to sprout again out at the Bunyip property?'

She shows us a photo, and there's green peeping in everywhere. My heart still aches at the space where the house once was, but if the birds and the bugs and the wombats are back then maybe everything's going to be all right.

The next morning, Hana and I walk across the 16th and the 5th arrondissements and cross the river at the Pont de la Tournelle. We video chat with our parents so they can see us together in front of (well, at the back of) the Notre Dame, its scaffolding supporting the restoration.

We eventually arrive at the Panthéon. It is cavernous and church-like. I'm not sure if it is, or was at some point in time, actually a church.

There is a column that reads: 'To the writers who died for France.' Antoine de Saint-Exupéry is buried here. We read *The Little Prince* at school in year seven so I know who Antoine de Saint-Exupéry is.

'I can't help thinking we'd never see this kind of monument back home,' whispers Hana.

I'd been thinking the same thing. First of all, which

writers would be willing to die for Australia? And second of all, I doubt the country would care so much about their sacrifice. Our heroes are sportspeople, soldiers, Aussie battlers. Artists are never battlers (except, of course, they are). Seeing an honour bestowed upon the people who worked to bring beauty to their country makes a little lump form in my throat. I don't think I'm particularly patriotic, but I want to believe I will have something to offer in my lifetime that will bring beauty to my country, my community. What will my country look like by the time I'm ready to beautify it? I'm still learning!

I suddenly realise that it is May, and I will be going home at the end of May. And I realise how, when I leave the *Arts Plastiques*, the class will go on to learn more techniques and styles and theories, and I won't because I'll be at home in Australia.

I am starting to dread it. What if I can never come back to Paris?

What am I going to submit for the exhibition?

How can we reverse climate change?

What will my future look like?

But I can't think about it.

I have to think about it.

In the middle of the Panthéon is Foucault's pendulum. It's a gold ball on the end of a long, long string or wire or something, and it demonstrates the earth's rotation.

It is hypnotic. We stand there – for I'm not even sure how long – and watch the world turn.

~

The next morning, Hana leaves.

'Headfirst,' she says, hugging me.

'Headfirst,' I reply.

35

At *Arts Plastiques*, my heart burns a little when I see Olivier, but not as much as it did before. I feel kind of sad for myself, but it's not even sadness so much as pity for him. It is just so disappointing! My heart burns with … not anger … but frustration and determination. Maybe the burning is my voice trying to come out.

I channel my frustration into working with new and different mediums.

Véronique recommended I look up American artist Keith Haring. In the 1980s he would go around the subway stations and draw speedy artworks on empty advertising spaces. He had to work fast, so he wouldn't get caught. 'He wouldn't lift his piece of chalk from the surface while he was drawing,' explained Véronique. 'Just one fluid line. I think practising this would be good for you.'

And so I have a go at chalk drawings on the ground. Maybe this is how I'll have my say! I start by re-creating some of my card sketches in the *cour* (courtyard) of Léon and Claudette's apartment, and the kids from the building come and dance around them. I let the kids use my chalk to do their own pictures.

I don't think I am close to being able to chalk in public, but maybe I am being too hard on myself. There's something to love about it as a medium. It's really vibrant if you choose the right colours.

Not only does it look fantastic, but it washes away. Perfect for someone like me who's trying to find her voice and figure out what she wants to say. If you mess it up, it won't last long. And if you change your mind about what it is you want to say, because you've learned something new or educated yourself better, that picture you made is long gone.

Chalk is the opposite of the internet.

Of course, someone may photograph your chalk drawing, post it online, and it could be seen by thousands, hundreds of thousands, millions of people, but that kind of stomps on my point.

Out on the streets there's protest afoot. 'We're going to make signs,' says Delphine. 'Want to come and help again?'

'Yes!' I reply. 'But do you want to help me with something on the way?' I try to keep a gleeful giggle out of my voice.

She rolls her eyes at me, but when I'm finished explaining she says, 'I'm in.'

We fill two plastic bags with pink paint. 'You just need to hold it like this,' I say, showing her how I've let my bag hang discreetly at my side.

Once we're outside we poke a hole in the bottom of each bag and let a line flow out as we jog towards the park, where her friends are meeting to finalise plans.

‘What’s the point of this again?’ Delphine asks.

‘Well,’ I start, ‘Debord says that the Spectacle is immune to subversion, right? I was looking at examples of culture jamming: like those Uncle Sam posters that actually say anti-American things. Or all the Obama posters. It’s satire, but it’s visual. It uses a well-known brand and takes aim at its intentions. Flips them on their head.’

‘Like an “Enjoy Capitalism” sign instead of “Enjoy Coca Cola”.’

‘Exactly!’ I say, and in my excitement I accidentally squeeze the bag and a big gloop of paint plops out. ‘Whoops. There are a lot of logo examples. But after a minute, these “subversive” things also lose their meaning. I just thought this might be a little less intentional, a little more permanent.’

‘I like it,’ says Delphine. ‘The Spectacle kind of acts like the immune system for late capitalism. We need to attack the system.’

I interpret that as we have to keep fighting! We have to work together. We have to create together. Tear it up together. *Sous les pavés, la plage!* Under the paving stones, the beach …

The line of paint marks the path from here to there, from me to we.

And what does it mean?

Absolutely nothing.

But it might get people thinking.

That refrain, now present in the back of my mind whenever I let it out from behind the dreamy good things: *remember, the world is ending/remember, the world is ending.*

Painting a meaningless line of pink paint along the footpath silenced the voice a little bit.

Making signs and getting ready for the protest helps more.

It's getting closer to summertime so we set up our sign-making station in the Luxembourg Gardens. I'm wearing a sleeveless dress – I'd put a skivvy on underneath it this morning, but the sun shone its beautiful face so I had to duck into some public loos to take it off.

We paint slogans – I paint the same one a couple of times and I can't help thinking of the possibilities of printmaking. Like the Atelier Populaire!

I plan to ask Véronique if the atelier has a screen-printing frame. I think I can make this happen.

36

When I wake up on the morning of the *manif* I have an exceptional amount of messages on my phone. All from one person.

Crow is absolutely buoyant.

The march went so well, she writes. *Even better than last time.* She's sent photo after photo and even video, and I watch the clips of passionate shouting under a clear Melbourne sky, and see the placards that read:

EXPLAIN TO FUTURE GENERATIONS 'IT WAS GOOD 4 THE ECONOMY!'

HOW MANY HUMANS DOES IT TAKE TO CHANGE THE GLOBE? (written within a drawing of a light globe)

CLIMATE EMERGENCY IN OUR SUNBURNT COUNTRY

And the one that smacks me right in the heart: *WHY STUDY FOR A FUTURE THAT WON'T EXIST?*

As I look, I begin crying in an unstoppable way that feels almost independent of my own body – no! Independent of my brain. It is just something my body has to do.

Crow's last message pings through: *Come on, Sof. Now it's your turn.*

In Paris in 1968, students and young people went on strike.

They were striking because of an outdated university system and a government they believed to be old-fashioned and behind the times. The strikes and the protests escalated. Within weeks this energy had gathered support from industry, and it wasn't long before strikes and protests stopped the entire country.

'My grandmother said people thought the war was back,' says Delphine. 'They were scared to go out to buy groceries. But the students were fighting for change.'

There's a French expression – *Plus ça change, plus c'est la même chose.* The more things change, the more they stay the same.

THIS.

When I first learned about May '68 it was the art that got me in. I was seduced by printmaking. Now I think I'm starting to understand the message, the drive – the urge to strike, to march, to speak.

Now we're in the present and this is my story, about the time I went to France. It was when the world was ending. The world had ended before, like the time when I was six and I called my prep teacher 'Mum'. Or when my nan died. Or when in year eight people were looking at me funny and I thought they were all laughing at me while I walked across the quad and I told myself not to be silly, but then Crow pointed out I had period blood on the back of my dress. Or when our house burned down.

This time it really feels like the world is ending on a grand scale. And look, I know that's happened before too. They even called World War I the 'war to end all wars', but really they were just warming up. Versions of this particular war have been going on the entire time I've been alive.

But now here we are. The sea levels are rising, the ice caps melting. Bushfire. Flood. Refugees escaping persecution, escaping famine, misery. We're smack-bang in the middle of something that feels suspiciously like the end of the world. It's a lot. And now my eyes can't unsee it. There's no beauty that can make me forget.

So here I go.

Headfirst.

Delphine and I dress for a day outside because we're not leaving the streets for anything. I've got my sturdiest boots on, and jeans, and a t-shirt I've painted myself with the words: *LA LUTTE CONTINUE.* The fight goes on. I have a big, thick woolly jumper in my bag in case I get cold. I feel strong in my outfit, and am happily surprised I find a feeling of beauty in this strength.

Delphine is humming with anger and determination. I've packed snacks into our pockets so she can keep it up.

A container of peanuts.

Some chocolate.

A bottle of water.

In 1968, factory workers ended up striking in solidarity with students, and they shut down half the country. Now, we are a crowd of thousands, gathering at the Place Saint-Michel. That site of youthful rebellion. We are young.

And not so young. We are angry, sad, desperate. We have three demands:

1. That governments declare a climate emergency.
2. That real action is taken on climate change and emissions.
3. That the people will be not only heard, but *listened to* by those in power.

I scroll through Instagram as we wait around, and Amandine has posted a photo of Olivier in the rally. His banner reads: *MAKE ART NOT EMISSIONS*. I'm embarrassed that he's toting around such a weak concept. But I scroll onwards and then he is gone from my mind.

There are brilliant, biting and true signs.

NIQUE PAS TA MER. Don't fuck your oceans.

QUAND C'EST FONDU, C'EST FOUTU. When it's melted, it's over.

LA PLANÈTE: TU LA VEUX BLEUE OU BIEN CUITE? Do you want your planet rare or well-done?

RÉFORME MON CUL. Reform my arse.

'That's one from 1968,' says Delphine as we start moving off as a group. It's magic to see the same slogans appear again. Time is cyclical. It's time to learn from our mistakes.

They tore up the cobblestone streets right here at the Place Saint-Michel, in 1968. The students built them up into barricades and torched cars, turning the Boulevard Saint-Michel into a battle zone. Now the streets we march along are smooth asphalt.

Lately I understand that need to upturn cars.

As we leave the square and walk past the Notre Dame and its scaffolding and sadness, someone links arms with me on one side – I look up surprised, and it's Delphine's long-haired friend, Manon.

'*Salut, Sofie,*' she says. She's wearing war paint under her eyes.

Manon's warm, assured camaraderie, and the way she smiles and shouts along with the crowd and the way she nods encouragingly, makes me feel brave, like I can take on the government and the elite with one solid stomp of my boot. I look to my other side, where people mill around, and I reach out.

I reach out and I take the arm of a girl who looks a little bit alone.

'Is this okay?' I shout and she smiles and we walk forward joined together.

I lift my face to the sky and I scream, and it's as though it comes from deep inside me. I don't know if anyone can hear me with all the shouting and movement on this street. I shout and I yell, and it feels like I'm wrestling hope from the fear and the desperation. Onward we march.

I hear, in a back little corner of my ear (*don't get too comfortable, remember the world is ending*), the sound of running feet. It starts quietly, but then it gets louder. Then there's voices too and people start running past. The tone of the shouting has changed. It's deeper, uglier.

A flame flies by my head, smashing with a glow and a ferociousness I hadn't expected, and there is so much shouting all of a sudden.

Masks and kerchiefs over faces.

Big, heavy work boots and black pants. Yellow vests.

The crowds surge and push.

What was once a joyful mass becomes chaos, and no-one is sure where to go.

All I can think is: *Don't get arrested, don't get deported, don't get smashed in the head by that policeman's nightstick, don't get shot don't get shot don't get shot …*

There is a guy staggering around and I run over. '*Vous êtes blessé?*' I shout. Are you hurt?

It's a warzone. I see Delphine out of the corner of my eye, making her way over.

The guy screams. It is a terrifying sound. *Where am I where am I where am I?* Everything is so loud. Another surge. I pull the guy by his jumper back towards the wall of a building, away from the road and the people.

Then a silver canister lands not too far away. Tear gas!

I turn my head, pulling my shirt up and over my face, my eyes already starting to itch, to stream tears, and I press myself into the stone wall.

I feel the guy disappear from beside me, and hear his boots scuffle across the footpath. I hope he'll be okay.

The surge has passed, the crowd is thinning and then there's the sound of high-pressure hoses. Water cannons. People are screaming and moving out of the way.

There's a shout from above. It's an angry Parisienne, and I can't tell if she's angry at me (at us) or angry at the world.

'The world is ending!' I shout, whether she can hear me or not. 'Won't you do something about it?'

Then Delphine is beside me. Her face is bright red and her whole head wet. Manon is on the other side. They take my hands in theirs and we run.

The boulevard is filled with upturned cars and paving stones, tear gas and sudden flames of homemade Molotov cocktails. Amid explosions and cries for *Macron démission*, cries for revolution, we run, our feet stumbling over rocks and iron grates from the street.

'Aren't you scared?' I ask Delphine.

Her eyes are bright. As she turns back towards the wreck and ruin, I can see flames reflected in her irises. 'What are you doing?' she screams. 'We're here to change the world!'

37

'Sofie, you need to give me a good reason not to send you home.' Toby sits across from me in the *salon* and his face is so serious. It had taken him just a few hours to see the images I'd posted of the protest, and to appear at the Durants' apartment.

It's like all the air has been sucked out of my body. 'I …' I begin. *I don't want to go home!* 'I had to take part. I want to have a future,' I say, and I hate that my voice wobbles.

Claudette is sitting quietly next to me and Delphine is perched on the arm of the sofa, while Léon stands by the door with his arms crossed. I take his pose as support for me.

Toby shifts in his seat. 'You will have a future.'

'You don't know that.'

He breathes out fast. 'Sofie, I get it. I'm scared too. But I've got a responsibility for all of you while you're here.'

I'm overwhelmed, and it isn't just about how I don't want to go home early. It's this feeling that maybe I don't want to go home *at all.*

'I know. And I'm sorry. We have our *Arts Plastiques*

exhibition in one week,' I plead. 'And after that it's really not long until the exchange is over. Please, Toby?'

He sighs. 'Will you promise me you'll stay out of trouble until then?'

I nod madly. 'I can do that.'

'There are rules you agreed to,' he says.

'To be fair, I didn't really read those rules,' I say, conspiratorially.

'Lalalala!' Toby covers his ears.

Out of the corner of my eye I see Delphine smirk.

In the end he agrees to pretend he never saw, and I agree to remove the photos and promise to stick to the rules for these last few weeks.

'I hope I haven't got you in trouble,' I say to my host parents after Toby has left. Some big tears threaten to break though.

Léon shakes his head. 'It will all work out,' he says.

'We've done nothing wrong,' says Delphine, angrily.

Claudette makes a gruff *ben, non* sound. 'My girl, you did worry us. You could have been hurt.'

When we'd got back to the apartment after the protest, we had to come clean. Delphine, with her tear-gassed red eyes, looked like she had been crying. But really she was halfway between celebrating and raging.

The *manifestation* gets in all the papers, and the coverage is positive towards the greenies and negative towards the *casseurs* who wreaked havoc once again on the streets.

Mum and Dad are torn between being super-duper worried, and kind of impressed and curious. Crow wants to know everything. Hana messages: *Do I need to come back from Greece and kick your bum? Btw I am so bloody proud of you.*

I feel engaged and also exhausted, but creatively satisfied. Or creatively motivated; like, I feel full of inspiration, even though we've been out all day and my knees hurt and my jeans are ripped and I've somehow got a cut on my head. A big egg and bruise is already forming, and Léon brings me some painkillers and a tea towel filled with ice.

I send a selfie to Hana. *I threw myself in headfirst.*

It is a moment of humour that is desperately needed.

However, later that week, my knees are starting to scab and itch, and the adrenaline has worn off. And there was a moment that flashed at me mid-protest, that made me turn around and gaze at the crowd, a moment that is coming to mean something.

Everyone was middle class.

There we were, shouting about climate action, poverty, about fairness and tax cuts for the rich – but we ARE the rich. We shout about climate justice, but what about the justice for the people of the Pacific Islands whose homes are being swallowed by our bloated seas (seas full of microplastics)? Taro Island in the Solomon Islands. It's predicted it will be the first capital city to face relocation as a result of the rise in sea levels.

And here I am, casually spending five months in another city, on the other side of the world. Taking long-haul flights that add enormous amounts of emissions into the atmosphere.

I feel Crow's despair now. I understand how she gets completely buried under the weight of the world. I feel different, but I also feel as though I have worked out a way to remain buoyant (to a degree) and not be dragged down. To enjoy the moment, to fight the small fights.

To own my anger, to recognise when and where it is useful.

I look at the maps I have made over the past five months. They all track the path from where I was to where I am now. They twist and they turn with the good times and the hard times.

Remember, the world is ending.

Delphine sends me a photo one of her friends had taken during the *manif.* In it, I'm standing in the middle of the street. For some reason the crowd has parted around me and I'm mid-shout. My hands are in fists by my side. I look wild. Both unlike myself and the most *myself* I have ever looked.

I want to upload it to Insta, to that Spectacle machine I still love using in spite of myself. Surely we can use it as a tool for good?

Is art important? When there are so many more immediate needs: water, food, shelter, a plan to preserve our ecosystem? But can't art bring change? It can change our emotions. We cry at the cinema; we are compelled to sing our favourite songs. Art is activism.

I feel energised to create; I am full of inspiration and bursting with feelings, experiences, opinions that just have to get out.

I want to create art that will make people think. I want my drawings and my paintings and my bizarre new linocut fascinations to mean something, to be something people can connect with.

Because if I can connect with people through my art and they can connect with me and with each other, then aren't we creating a community? And if we have a community even five people strong, we are stronger together and we'll get things done.

The Society of the Spectacle says that even when people create *détournements* (hijackings) to try and break out of the Spectacle, the Spectacle co-opts them and absorbs the *détournement* back into the Spectacle. Just like when teenagers create a new slang expression or a new way of wearing a hat or something, and there's marketing departments following them around ready to co-opt the word or the look and sell it back to the same teenagers. It is exhausting.

I feel angry again at Olivier for making a map of a girl for his exhibition, for co-opting *me*.

I look over all my maps out at once. My favourite is a world map. I've used an actual world map for this one, not a woodcut print. I've marked a path from Melbourne to Paris, with all the places Crow thinks about and despairs over: Nauru, Myanmar, Syria, Sudan. I've called it *As the Crow Flies*.

Véronique has been nudging me in the direction of artists she thinks I'll connect to – many with collage-illustration, abstraction, loose lines she thinks I can capture. I do like the way Jean-Michel Basquiat puts small illustrations together on canvas or paper to make one big piece. It's less overwhelming, and I can see how I could do something similar. My pieces are interconnected.

I look at the posters I made for Crow all those months ago and I am surprised at the level of anger they contain. I almost feel afraid this anger came from me. I could probably try to explain it away as me channelling her anger for this commission.

But, truth be told, I did feel angry. I do feel angry.

And now, after everything that has happened, I feel ready to use my anger.

To use my anger for good.

38

BREAK A LEG!

– Overnight chats with Crow

The exhibition. We each get to choose four pieces to show, and I finally decide on my pieces the day before. After everything, they are so much more personal than I realised, and I'm happier about each of them than I had expected to be.

The night before the art show I dream in French. It is the first time I have dreamed in French and when I wake up, I wake up crying even though the dream wasn't sad.

I was dreaming about flying. Not in an aeroplane, but like a bird, though I *think* I was human still. And I flew over Paris. At least I think it was Paris. I flew over the city, then over green fields to an ocean, and then I flew over that as though something was guiding my way. My black feathered wings (because in dreams humans can have crows' wings) beat confidently. We know where to go.

We have to be there early to set up, and it's a particular

trip on the metro carrying my pieces under my arm. Our *Arts Plastiques* class has been allocated its own exhibition space within the École des Beaux-Arts for this occasion. It's a large white room with only one window at the front and you enter into it from the large courtyard in the middle of the building.

We hang our art the way we want it to be seen and I've chosen not to frame mine. Véronique tuts and *ppts* a little as I try to explain my rationale:

'It's like, this one is a map,' I say. 'Like a map for walking the road and finding the places you search for.' Talking about my own art can be tricky at the best of times – but it's doubly hard in another language. 'These maps are for all the world—' I wave my hands around expansively to illustrate 'the world'. 'If you put them in a frame, then nobody can touch them, or walk around to find the places you search for. I don't want to contain them.'

Véronique does one of those shrug-*bof* things and moves on to the next student.

I look up at my work. Without frames they almost bleed into the walls. The edges of the maps aren't perfectly straight and I've folded and unfolded them before putting them up. For extra authenticity.

Yes, I decided to include my maps in spite of everything. I've printed three. A map of Paris, with all the shiny landmarks marked in pristine photographic glory. A second identical map, with the same landmarks as the first, but with additional features in printed linocut. A dot for 'home' in Belleville and thick black paths to school, to the metro, to the top of the Belleville hill. A third map, additionally marked in bright pink ink – a love map of all the places Olivier and I walked. Yet another, marked at the points where the camps were destroyed, where the protest route was, the community garden where we gave soup to those who needed soup: places where plans were flourishing in secret.

I want to make a digital version of these maps too, sometime. I could overlay each version like archaeology in motion, but instead of stripping away the layers of history, I'd be adding them, mapping my path through place and time.

For my fourth piece, though, I've brought the largest of my cardboard collages. On it I've stuck our placards and posters from the rally, overlapping like they're pasted on a wall somewhere. I've printed over the top of them – words and shapes for effect. If you look down the bottom there's a sheet of paper featuring a strange creature. Our exquisite corpse.

It's a style still in development. Maybe I should have exhibited one of my pears (they *are* very pear-ish these days) – but I LIKE this one. I steal a slogan from '68 as its title: *I Have Something To Say But I Don't Know What.*

I believe art and life are inextricable and there is horror and beauty in everything. And we can have both. We can be both.

Claudette, Léon and Delphine come along, of course. I feel incredibly nervous about this. I feel such strange, strong feelings towards this family who aren't my family. They have been here, hovering in the background for almost five months – making sure I didn't starve and that

I came home every night and felt as safe as possible in this adopted city of mine.

Claudette stands with her hands on her hips and looks at my work. She points to the cardboard piece, shaking her finger approvingly (her bangles clinking together cheerily). 'I like this. I am happy you've taken a risk and created something unconventional. But I suppose I shouldn't be surprised. You are a very interesting young woman.'

'I agree,' says Léon, and the way he looks at my pieces, nodding his head with a little smile on his face, says more than words.

I wonder if Léon felt as observed at his *vernissage* or if this slightly uncomfortable naked feeling goes away. While Léon hasn't been a mentor in the way Véronique has, I feel like I've learned a lot from him about the multitudes of being an artist.

I watch my host parents walk slowly around the exhibition, greeting people they know and talking low to each other while pointing and gesturing at the artworks.

I also happen to be watching when Olivier puts his arm around a girl who is wearing a silky slip of a dress and long, delicate silver earrings. She is waifish and beautiful. I feel envious, and then furious at myself.

'What are you going to wear?' Delphine had asked that morning, leaning against my doorway, looking as nonchalant as only Delphine can look.

'I don't know. It's not so important, is it?' I lied. It was terribly important to me, and I was worried I wouldn't look the part, that I wouldn't look good.

'*Bah, comme t'es fatigante!*' I had heard Claudette say this very phrase to Delphine like it was an automatic reaction, and I had to laugh hearing it come out of Delphine's very own mouth. Oh, you're exhausting!

We went into Delphine's room and she wrenched open her wardrobe, which was bursting with things. 'I took some of these from *maman*, of course …'

She dressed me in a simple shift dress with a geometric pattern across the hem. 'You are going to look like a picture. Stand right in front of his face and be your beautiful self.'

'You realise I broke up with him?' I asked. 'It's the art I'm angry about.'

She shrugged. *Bof.* 'This will help anyway.'

I've never worn this shade of red before, but it's a colour that says *I have something to say.*

I watch Olivier stand next to his pieces. They're framed in gold frames, if you can believe it, and I want to vomit with the pot-calling-the-kettle-sell-out. He's achieved what he wanted with mood and style: deep, gloomy oil paints of Romanticism, but featuring young people on their phones and wearing branded clothing. The paintings are very beautiful, which is frustrating for me.

Then there's the map series – a face (my face), the palm of a hand (my hand), the sole of a foot (is that my foot?) – painted over with a fine gold line. A dot indicating 'start here' and the line spreading out across the image, giving it the feel of Japanese Kintsugi. The triptych is called *Connaître* (*To Know*). I'm surprised to see that while the final products are interesting, and certainly technique-wise they're stunning and envy-inducing, they feel a bit empty.

Léon stands on one side of me, Véronique on the other.

'It's interesting enough,' Léon says. 'Skillful brushwork.' I can feel him looking over my head to Véronique.

From the corner of my eye I see her mouth pout and her shoulders shrug lightly. 'It's missing some soul. I suspect he's trying to capture something he doesn't fully understand. Theoretically, and in terms of subject.'

I try not to feel too triumphant.

Claudette and Léon work the room – speaking to this person and that, laughing and touring the artworks together. I'm happy to stand away from the crowd with Delphine, our backs to the wall and our shoulders touching. She bumps against me gently. 'It's good,' she says, nodding towards my work.

I bump her back. 'Thank you.'

I see us as if in a photo: her in a crisp white t-shirt tucked into black high-waisted trousers, her bony limbs with their sharp angles (not model-thin, like I had thought at first, but marathon-ready, with endurance and strength), and me in a borrowed dress.

Véronique comes over. 'Sofie, I am very proud of you.' She kisses me, *mwah mwah*. Then, to top it off, Léon buys one of my pieces. I watch him have a conversation with Véronique and soon after a red dot is placed next to the Belleville map.

My heart!

39

Véronique asks me if she can take me for a goodbye visit to a brasserie. 'May I invite you?' she asks, and I know these days that 'to invite' someone means 'to shout' them. I feel a kind of happiness and pride, and a number of other things at once: delight that she cares enough to meet me outside of class, and a mature headiness at the thought of having a friend out of my age group. Crow and her granny have such a great relationship, and it's always felt unfair that young people and older people aren't encouraged to socialise.

People might think Véronique and I are mother and daughter, or aunt and niece, perhaps, as we walk from the Saint-Germain-des-Prés metro stop. No, I'd say, we're *friends*.

I am casual, carefree, letting my jacket flap open to the elements because winter is well and truly done, done, done. She is wearing a blousy scarf, all silky and floral printed. Effortless chic. I still have not attained it – perhaps it comes with age.

Before I came to Paris a part of me felt it was a bit touristy and cliché to go to a brasserie. Of course I still *wanted* to do it, desperately, and it filled at least one corner of my daydreams. But I love that the reality of life in France is that you *do* go to brasseries – you can stand at the bar and quickly drink your *café express*, or you can sit on one of the chairs (yes, wicker, cane, whatever they're made of – probably some kind of plastic these days) and spend time watching the world go by.

Except this morning is different. Véronique and I don't go to any old brasserie. We go to the Deux Magots. Véronique takes me to the Deux Magots!

'Voila,' she says, as we sit down on wicker chairs at one of the outside tables. '*On est bien là.* Everyone should go to the most famous *brasserie* in Paris at least once in their life.'

'Do you know who used to come here?' I ask, trying to keep a wondrous, disbelieving tone out of my voice.

'But of course. Sartre. Simone de Beauvoir.' She is matter-of-fact.

A waiter in a full black suit with a crisp white shirt and apron takes our order.

Once he's walked away, I say excitedly, 'Yes, exactly! Hemingway!'

'Julia Child.'

That one makes me laugh.

Our coffees come carried on a tray and are set down with a flourish. Each one comes with a little chocolate with the café's logo on it, which I like very much and immediately put in my pocket as a souvenir.

'*Tu veux une cigarette?*' asks Véronique, while we wait for our food. She pulls a very fancy pack of slim cigarettes out of her pocket.

'I don't usually smoke,' I say.

There's a little pack of matches sitting on our table – again, emblazoned with the logo – as though if you strike a match at the Deux Magots you might just strike Jean-Paul Sartre back into being (although what would he know?).

'But I would quite like to try,' I explain. 'Is that okay?'

She lights the match and puts it to the cigarette. Inhales. 'But of course.'

She pushes the packet across to me, then turns her head to exhale, the smoke wafting away. She taps the ash into the ashtray.

I reach over and take a cigarette, rolling it between my fingers. Then I bring the cigarette to my mouth and already I hate the way it feels and tastes on my lip. I strike the match. As I light the cigarette and wave the match quickly back and forth to extinguish it – for this brief moment – I exist across time. I am a painting, I am fiction, I am a brief flash of light.

I inhale, cough the smoke back out. 'That's really very disgusting.'

We both start laughing. I like Véronique's gravelly deep laugh.

I rest the cigarette in the ashtray. I know I won't go back to it.

'Are you looking forward to going home in Australia?' she asks, in English.

I smile inside at her little mistake – or, rather, quirk of translation; we have never spoken English together before and maybe I thought she didn't know how. It's nice to be surprised.

'Sort of,' I say, and it's the closest to the truth I can get for now. 'I miss my family.' Again, truth. 'But I am going to miss my life here. I feel like I've changed a lot. Inside.'

She doesn't say anything, and I'm not really sure what I expect or want her to say. She hasn't yet touched her coffee.

'Were you happy with the exhibition?' Véronique asks, and all the emotions from the day rush through me again: pride, anxiety, gratitude.

'It was more than I had hoped for,' I say. 'It felt very special. Thank you for everything.'

'I am impressed, Sofie, with the way you have developed your work since you arrived. You're producing more confident pieces, and exploring different methods and styles. I received very positive comments from friends and colleagues on your pieces.'

My heart leaps with ego and possibility. *Very positive comments!* Maybe there is a future for me. Maybe there is a future for my art.

'Keep challenging yourself. Keep experimenting – you cannot fail if you work hard. You do want to come back to Paris to study?' she asks, staring down at me through her half-moon glasses with red plastic frames. 'Is that something you have been thinking about?'

I don't reply straight away, but I nod my head. My fingers dart across my lap, nervous. 'Yes,' I say. 'Yes, that is something I want to do.'

We share a look. It feels important. I feel like I'm becoming someone new.

Véronique stubs her cigarette out. 'Good.'

But we don't discuss it further.

She says nothing about the cigarette I left to smoke itself out in the ashtray. A good reminder to let people try new things with no expectations.

'Goodbye, Sofie,' Véronique says, and we give *les bises.* 'Until next time.'

Delphine and I meet to take a walk through the Cimitière du Montparnasse. The cemetery is not a gloomy place to be. It's filled with respect and flowers and trees.

I don't make a map of this cemetery today because there's one right here with everything I need. A map to show you where Serge Gainsbourg is (singer – his grave covered in metro stubs and flowers and cigarette butts), Marguerite Duras (writer – her grave is decorated with pens!), Alfred Dreyfus (*'J'accuse!'* says Delphine, and I vow to look it up later), or Charles Baudelaire.

Delphine wants to show me the grave of Jean-Paul Sartre and Simone de Beauvoir. 'They're buried together. It's sickeningly romantic. You'll love it.'

The gravestone is plain, though there are flowers and trinkets on it.

'It is romantic,' I say slowly. 'But maybe I'm not drawn to romance as much as I once was.' It's dazzling to think how much I've changed after five months, one doomed relationship, one political awakening and fifty million croissants.

We sit on a park bench, surrounded by the past and so many lives lived – lived well, lived poorly, lived short and long – and the day is so beautiful and so perfect, and if I were still a romantic I'd want to kiss someone in this cemetery under the springtime trees. I will find someone to kiss, sometime, probably. I don't know who they are yet, and I'm not in a hurry.

'What should we do now?' Delphine asks. 'It's your last day in Paris.'

'And on such a beautiful day, let's just sit here a little longer.' I don't get my phone out. My fingers don't draw patterns on my knee. I just sit back on the bench, with birdsong and sunlight.

But although Delphine and I sit quietly, our sitting with each other is important. She pulls a paperback book out of her jacket pocket – like a character in a movie, I kid you not – and she bumps my shoulder softly and I bump her back, then she settles in to read.

I watch the new green leaves on the trees wink and wave in the light, listen to the faint chatter of tourists searching for the particular headstone they have come to find, watch a city worker dressed all in green replace the bag in a nearby bin. I don't know if I've mentioned it before now but a lot of public bins in Paris are just short basketball hoops with transparent green bin bags attached. Am I ruining this moment by thinking about garbage? No. Garbage can be beautiful too.

The sun is shining, the sky is blue, I am so happy to be in this beautiful city, and even happier I know how to appreciate and accept its complexities of beauty. And I'm happy to be with Delphine, this new friend who has, over five short months, become so important to me.

This moment is magnificent. It is fireworks and soaring orchestral music. It is like looking at the *Winged Victory* for hours and it is beating my own wings to fly.

I hope we will know each other forever.

I am ready to go home now.

I am ready to work hard.

I am ready to have my voice heard.

Sofie

I think my phone is listening to me.

Crow

Yes, it is. I've told you this.

D and I visited JP Sartre's grave yesterday
and now I keep getting recommended quotes.

I don't think that's your biggest issue.

How's this: 'There may be more beautiful
times, but this one is ours.'

...

Crow?

Yeah. I feel that one.

– Overnight chats with Crow

Then, suddenly, it is my last morning in Paris. The view from my bedroom window is just as grey as the day

I arrived, but I glory at the sight. I fly out at 2 pm.

When I landed in France those few months ago, I felt so grown up, like I was a child who had been turned out into the world. Now, after everything that's happened, it is as though I've lived a thousand lives. I've forgotten everything, learned it again, and then realised I was wrong.

I feel part of the world in a way I don't think I have before. In fact I know I haven't.

The *famille* Durant take me out. We go to the top of the Tour Montparnasse because I haven't gone before. More than one person has said I should go to the top of the Montparnasse tower because you get the best view of Paris – purely because the ugly tower *isn't in that view!* The lift is ear-popping and we're surrounded by tourists – and I don't feel like a tourist.

We take a photo of us all together using an automatic postcard stand that costs two euros a go. You can choose a frame and other decoration. Léon thinks it is hilarious and digs around in his pocket for more coins. 'One for you, and one for us,' he says.

I can see the Parc de Belleville.

I can see the Sacré Cœur.

Everywhere I turn there is something new to see as well.

I panic a bit when I realise how much of Paris I haven't seen yet – let alone the rest of the country, the world, the universe.

'I should have gone for a walk through the Bois de Boulogne,' I say to Delphine.

'When you come back we can run through it,' she says.

When I come back. I wonder if coming back to Europe is a possibility. I have been thinking a lot about my giant climate footprint.

'Maybe I won't ever come back,' I say. 'Maybe when the climate revolution comes, they'll ground all aeroplanes. International travel will be something we just talk about, like, "Remember when …?" as we walk and ride and train our grandchildren around.'

'Maybe.' Delphine leans against the railing, the Eiffel Tower behind and below her. 'I don't think I will even have children, let alone grandchildren. But if I do, what will their lives be like?'

It is easy to be incredibly frightened when thinking about the world.

I circle the viewing deck many times, taking in all the angles of the city.

Over there is the Panthéon. There the Gare du Nord. Les Invalides.

I think about Haussmann and the way he redesigned Paris to give it form and function, but how in order to do so he had to destroy homes and cemeteries and disrupt life. It must have been terrible for everyone living here at that time. They would have felt like their world was ending.

This city is like an onion with its layers of human joy and misery and if you wander with an open mind and open eyes, you'll see them.

Maybe the whole world is like that.

I take photos. I think about posting some. I don't. I might later because my Insta has become a place to record my history; it's become a map of its own, marking the way I've moved through the world and the way I've looked at it.

Faces, places, wide open spaces.

So now. Now I'm going to take my open mind and open eyes home. I can't wait to see home with this new vision.

I have something to say, and I'm starting to learn what that is.

Delphine puts her whole self into what she believes in, channelling her worry and energy into music and activism.

Léon allows himself to dream (by bringing nightmares to life).

Claudette sees the best way to get through reality to make dreams happen.

Crow and I have plans.

Poster plans and talking plans and action plans.

I see more beauty than ever – in people, places, things – and I see beauty in the broken and the dirty and the lost. It's a revelation. I glory in the messy and the uncomfortable. It's nothing to be afraid of. It's easy to be overwhelmed, but I trust my feet, my arms, my heart and my mind.

At least I think I do.

I feel like I'm at the start of something frightening and exciting.

The world might be ending, but we're only just beginning.

Author's Note

The title of this book comes from a quote attributed to Jean-Paul Sartre. I have searched in English and French but haven't, at the time of printing, been able to pin down the source. But it was so perfect and rang around my head as I wrote, so I want it to be real. Allegedly, it goes like this:

My dear

There may be more beautiful times, but this one is ours.

Look back, look forth, look close, there may be more prosperous times, more intelligent times, more spiritual times, more magical times, and more happy times, but this one, this small moment in the history of the universe, this is ours.

And let's do everything with it. Everything.

Falsely yours,

Jean-Paul Charles Aymard Sartre

See what I mean? And there were four books that I used most in the writing and the rewriting of this book: Guy Debord's 1967 *La Société du spectacle* – though I also read it in English as *The Society of the Spectacle*, where it was only slightly less difficult to understand; Greta Thunberg's book of speeches, *No One Is Too Small to Make a Difference*; Asger Jorn and Guy Debord's artists' book, *Mémoires*; and *Beauty is in the Street: A visual uprising of the May 68 uprising* by Johan Kugelberg with Philippe Vermès (ed).

I couldn't have written the book without The Art Assignment, Paul Taylor's videos for French language hilarities, Jay Swanson's YouTube channel for seeing what the weather was doing in Paris on any given day, and Paris 68 Redux on Insta for framing the posters of the Atelier Populaire in a modern context.

Though I have been back since, my experience living in France was village life in the Lot region circa 2006. My days were spent driving three children around in a Renault station wagon, singing Louise Attaque and the Magic Numbers. I attended zero protests, unless you count the kids protesting against eating one savoury crêpe for dinner before moving on to Nutella.

This book is set in the months between January and May 2019. I have gleefully spliced real events with made-up ones, and real places with made-up or misremembered ones. All errors are my own.

Acknowledgements

Thank you, Kristina Schulz, Clair Hume and Cathy Vallance at UQP, for being so patient and supportive as I took so much time to finish this book. I feel very lucky to have had Melissa Keil work on the copyedit – thank you for getting it, and for making it better. Thank you, Vanessa Lanaway, for the proofread. Thank you, Astred Hicks, for another kickarse cover.

Thank you, Beck Bergin, for leaping with me when you or I thought: *Why not move to France and get jobs?* Thank you to Emmanuelle Vauché, and Katline, Tony and Kevin Demeulemeester, to whom this book is dedicated, for giving me a home in Martel. I feel very lucky to know you all, and to have watched you three grow up to be such politically engaged, socially conscious global citizens.

How can I repay you, Beth Herwood, for always opening your house, and your Montmartre bars, to me? Or Aurélie and Vincent, and Baptiste and Émilie, who take time for me, feed me, and expand my vocab whenever I visit?

Thank you to Lena O'Donnell, Hannah Cartmel and Lauren Maserow for sharing your experiences of going on foreign-language exchange trips. I wish I could have used more of your anecdotes and mistakes, but your truths are too strange for fiction.

Thank you to Kate Russell and Clare Humphries for helping me land on a title when I circled around it for ages, and for reminding me that singing together makes everything good again, even when you're on a deadline.

I am so grateful to Lili Wilkinson and Vikki Wakefield for the ego-boosting endorsements.

And dear Sun Bookshop, and The Younger Sun, I love you – and all who work and have worked in you. As I write this, things are very strange, and I hope by the time this book comes out, our doors are open again, and we're ready for a party.

Pandemics aside, our times are still strange, with our planet in peril and our futures uncertain. But while we're here, in our 'small moment in the history of the universe', let's make noise, make art, and make change.

Also by Kate O'Donnell
UNTIDY TOWNS

Shortlisted for the Indie Book Awards
Shortlisted for the Readings Young Adult Book Prize

Seventeen-year-old Adelaide is sick of being expected to succeed on other people's terms. She knows she just has to stick it out at school for one more year and then she'll be free. Instead, she runs away from her fancy boarding school back to her sleepy hometown to read and dream.

But there are no free rides. When Addie's grandad gets her a job at the local historical society, she soon finds out that it's dusty and dull, just like her new life. Things change when she starts hanging out with Jarrod, a boy who seems full of possibilities. But it turns out he's as stuck as she is. And Addie realises that when you want something in life, you've actually got to do something about it.

Written with heart and humour, this gorgeous tale will leave you smiling. – Fiona Wood

I adored this book, with its gorgeous prose and characters I didn't want to leave behind. – Cath Crowley

ISBN 978 0 7022 5982 1

UQP